Catch AND Release

THE INSIDERS' GUIDE TO Alaska Men

by

Jane Haigh

Kelley Hegarty-Lammers

Patricia Walsh

HILLSIDE PRESS, FAIRBANKS • RIDGETOP PRESS, HOMER
ALASKA

Thank you to all of our friends who shared
their insights, antics, and stories!

An original publication of Ridgetop Press
P.O. Box 1521 • Homer, AK 99603-1521
907-235-5431 • akplaces@alaska.net

Second Edition, June 1997.
A publication of Hillside Press, Fairbanks, Alaska.
For information contact Hillside Press
280 E. Birch Hill • Fairbanks, AK 99712
907-457-7834 • FAX: 907-457-7835 • jhaigh@polarnet.com

ISBN: 0-9627530-2-5

Printed in the U.S.A.

about this book

How Are We Writing This Book?
It's all being done with duct tape and mirrors, typical Alaskan fashion.

Why Are We Writing This Book?
Someone had to do it! Besides, faced with another long cold, dark, winter, we needed to do something to entertain ourselves.

Where Are We Writing This Book?
All over Fairbanks on bootlegged computer time, at *Bun on the Run* and over cappuccino at *Hot Licks*.

Who Are We?
In other words, why the heck should you take our advice? Do we really know what we're talking about?

We are three friends, originally from the East Coast, the West Coast and the Midwest, who have over fifty years combined experience living, working, and playing in Alaska. We have traveled this state from top to bottom, side to side, coast to coast.

Between our own experiences and those of our friends, we've heard all the lines, been wooed by all the drama of all the lifestyles, and had all the adventures. It was just that sense of adventure and romance that brought us to Alaska and it's why we have chosen to stay. Trust us.

Dedicated
To the Men of Alaska

"If we didn't like Alaska men, we wouldn't be here."
Pat, Kelley, and Jane

Catch AND Release

THE INSIDERS' GUIDE TO **Alaska Men**

Understanding The Alaska Man

A humorous look at the development of the Alaska man
from the first men who crossed the Bering Land Bridge
10,000 years ago through the rise of aviation, which added
the all important bush pilot to the ranks of Alaska men, to
the pipeline that significantly swelled their numbers.

A list from 'A-architect' to 'Z-zoologist' with a pithy
paragraph on each distinctive type of the species.

The Meet Of The Matter

The prime fishing spots - from the bars to the docks - where to go to meet Alaska men (if you still want one that is) and which type you are most likely to find where. This section covers each region of Alaska and includes an introductory paragraph on the major towns and cities and some critical places in between.

Courtship With The Alaska Man

Every Alaska man has his sport or, more likely, sports. From ice fishing to hockey, kayaking to skiing and ice climbing, they take their sports seriously. Their women should come along, come prepared, and be ready to cope with the elements. It's a test. Should you choose to compete, this chapter will help you pass.

You can't have a book about Alaska men without a chapter on Sex.

Survival Tools

how to use this book

Just by purchasing this book, you've taken that all important first step toward meeting the Alaska man of your dreams. So, chuck the cruise brochure, and after reading *The Meet of the Matter*, pick out one or two spots that appeal to you. Plan on spending a few weeks getting to know people. Relax, this will involve healthy amounts of hanging out.

Then, check out our *Guide to the Lifestyles*, so you'll know what kind of guys you'll be likely to meet and what they are about. For example, suppose you've made it as far as the Red Dog Saloon in Juneau. Having followed our advice, you're dressed in a matching outfit so everyone will know that you're new in town. You spot that gorgeous hunk you've been looking for and he asks you to sit down. Having

memorized our instructions, you order an Alaska Pale Ale. He tells you he's a fisherman. You go to the ladies room and surreptitiously look up "fisherman" under "F" in our exclusive "Guide to the Lifestyles." There you quickly review our suggestions, emerging to ask him an intelligent question. "So, what kind of boat do you have...a seiner or a bow picker?" Having memorized our fishing industry information, you know that when he answers "a bow picker" you're talking to the low fisherman on the totem pole, and you can politely excuse yourself before you get in too deep.

Or suppose you manage to get as far as Unalaska on the Aleutian chain by following our advice to increase your odds. Hanging out on the docks making watercolor sketches, you are not a bit surprised when a tall, dark, mysterious looking blue-eyed stranger in a coarse wool sweater looks over your shoulder and says "Kak-Dayla." You already know that this is the port for the Russian fishing fleet and the most endearing response you could possibly make is pronounced "hara-show." What could be more exotic?

Or you have made it to the Howling Dog Saloon in Fairbanks on a June Friday night at the height of the midnight sun. In fact, you arrive at the fashionable hour of midnight, after taking a nap as per our instructions. While playing volleyball out in the corral, you get talking to the tall blond guy in high tops, and he says he's building his own cabin. At least you now have sense enough not to be immediately impressed; rather, as we suggest, you ask how long he's been working on it, if he has plans to finish it, and even more importantly, if he has a job. If you don't like his answers, you can look for a university professor who will likely be sitting next to you at the bar anyway.

Moving right along, after casing the local hang outs on the trip up from Juneau through Anchorage and Fairbanks, you've finally met your ideal Alaska guy after following our advice and traveling to Arctic Circle Hot Springs Resort in time for clean-up on the gold creeks. (After checking the glossary, you know that

"clean-up" refers to the process of recovering the gold from the sluicing equipment.) Your guy is a placer miner, and he invites you to meet him in Fairbanks for a fishing trip following the mining season.

Luckily, having read our section on *Sports and Activities*, you head right for Big Ray's Sporting Goods in Fairbanks. You know now that you need a few good flannel shirts, some rain gear and a pair of sturdy rubber boots - appropriate clothing for sitting in the mud and cleaning fish. You know that no matter how much he appreciated your attractive touring outfits at the hot springs, what an Alaska man really likes is a woman who comes prepared to cope with the elements.

You pass the outdoors training inspection, and he invites you to come home with him. After perusing our instructional bachelor cabin illustrations, you're prepared to confront his *"home."* This is good, because instead of registering total shock and dismay, you can express pleasant surprise that it's not as bad as some of our examples. This positive attitude will be greatly appreciated by your suitor.

Yes, Alaska is a land of adventure and romance. It has touched and captured each of us. So, come prepared to have fun. Don't be in too much of a hurry, relax, and have a good time!

Understanding
The
Alaska
Man

CHAPTER 1

a historical perspective on Alaska bachelors

It all started some ten thousand years ago, when the first Alaska Man came trudging over the Bering Land Bridge to the far northwest corner of Alaska. Anthropologists have long puzzled over the question of why Early Man made this journey eastward, and you may wonder just what that prehistoric Alaska man has to do with the rugged and handsome heroes of today's last frontier. We are here to tell you that even this very primitive version of Alaska Man made the arduous journey into unknown lands in search of adventure and romance. In short, he did it because he needed to sow some wild oats and he wanted a good hunting story to tell his buddies. Of course, have you ever heard anything about Early Women crossing the land bridge, or the settlements of Early Woman in Alaska? No, of course not. It's only Early Man who had these exploits. So, where did early Alaska Man find early Alaska Woman? Good question!

B.C.   Bering Land Bridge
Primitive Alaska man travels from eastern Siberia
to northwestern Alaska in search of adventure and
romance, hoping to return with a good hunting
story to tell his buddies.

1835   Whalers and Traders Visit Alaska
These are, of course, men. They discover that Alaska's inhabitants are into
free love, finding a culture on the cutting edge of a sexual revolution that
didn't reach San Francisco for another 130 years.

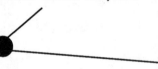

1849   The California Gold Rush
Ice and singles ads are shipped
from the Russian Capital of Sitka
to the new city of San Francisco.
Brides and the latest in sports
equipment are the return cargo.

1880   The Founding of Juneau
Joe Juneau and Dick Harris
discover gold in Juneau, and an
unknown Alaska hero establishes
the first bar. The early gold miners
find easy gold, and the sporting
girls find easy pickings. In 1900 the
capital was moved to Juneau, and
with the creation of the first
legislature, the legislative party
animal was created.

10,000 B.C.   First Village Site
Anthropologists tell us that men and women lived in comparative harmony in these early times, sharing the work of the household and child-rearing, as well as hunting and gathering to procure food. Alaska woman has been striving ever since to return to those happy times, while Alaska man has been looking ever since for an even better hunting story to tell his buddies.

1741   Russian Discovery
The first sighting of an Alaska man by Commander Vitus Bering in the Shumagin Islands of the Aleutian Chain. The man is observed hunting, an endeavor he pursues even today.

1800   Russian Settlement
The Russians settle Kodiak, Sitka and the Aleutians with men. Very few Russian women come to the new world. Thus, the pattern of self centered Euro-Alaska Bachelors was established in the beginning of the 19th century.

1898   The Klondike Gold Rush
An unprecedented influx of men, and a few women, move into the otherwise sparsely settled interior of Alaska and the Yukon. With the attendant publicity which the goldrush attracts, the myth of the rugged Alaska man is born. Ready to tackle any adventure, endure any risk, in search of gold or a good story to tell his buddies, the Alaska man soon assumes larger than life proportions.

1920   Early Aviation

The coming of aviation is a watershed in the development of Alaska resources, but this event is overshadowed by the fact that the first planes make possible the first Alaska bush pilots, forever enhancing the myth of the rugged Alaska man.

1910   Early settlement

The typical Alaska prospector hikes out across the many miles of rolling hills in search of gold in an elusive creek bottom. Establishing his claim, he continues to prospect for the mother lode, while Alaska woman builds the cabin, plants the garden, hunts and butchers moose and caribou, harvests and cans garden produce, mushes 20 miles for firewood and two hundred miles for flour, butter, and sugar. She entertains his buddies while they swap hunting stories.

1950   Homesteading

World War II veterans stake their homesteads, and go hunting, while the wife clears and plants the north forty, builds a cabin, plants the garden, tends the animals, bakes, cooks, and entertains his buddies while they swap hunting and war stories.

1960   The Sixties

The sixties never happened in Alaska, until the seventies. Maybe that's why Alaska Men think of the sixties as the good old days, before women's lib, before the pipeline, before steady jobs, before inflation, before mortgages, and before all those newcomers spoiled the hunting and fishing.

1975   The Pipeline Years

This was the modern heyday of the Alaska man, his numbers and mythological proportions swelled by fat rolls of hundred dollar bills in his pocket, enhanced by the new jargon of camps and pump stations and belly dumps and seven-twelves.

1930   Tourist Destination
Alaska soon becomes a tourist destination for thousands of early 20th Century American women in search of adventure and a rugged Alaska man.

1942   World War II
In Alaska, World War II multiplied logarithmically the number of Alaska men. Simultaneously, the myth of the Alaska man was further puffed up with an infusion of military machismo, and the war story was added to the repertoire that could be traded around the camp fire.

1942   The Alaska Highway
Built in nine months over some of the most rugged terrain on the continent, the AlCan Highway further enhances the can-do machismo of the Alaska man and provides direct overland access for women to pursue them.

1980   The Eighties: Alaska Goes Bust
Reaganomics and conservatism promotes the attractiveness of rugged individualism, but the economic bust caused by falling oil prices decreases the number of Alaska men. With an increase ratio of women to men, is the Alaska man becoming an endangered species? Not a chance.

1990   The '90s
Men in the Lower 48 states rediscover their maleness by retreating to the nearest state park and beating on drums. Alaska men, on the other hand, buy ever more powerful snow machines, and dream up even more bizarre sports and competitions, such as the Iditabike, extreme skiing, and the Wilderness Classic.

CHAPTER 2

insiders' guide to the lifestyles

*An exclusive compendium of types, how to recognize them,
what to expect, and how to be prepared.*

This is a very important component of our little book. If that gorgeous Hunk next to you at the public hearing on timber harvests says he's a *'fisherman'*, well, what does that mean? Does he spend his time with a rod and reel beside a scenic trout stream? Let us help you figure it out. Just turn to our handy guide under "F", and you'll find out more than you ever wanted to know about these guys - some helpful hints about his lifestyle and livelihood, as well as some conversational tips about the type of gear he runs. Learn to recognize the various types of boats, which boats are likely to belong to wealthy as opposed to poverty-line fishermen. So pay attention now!

> *"...the odds are good, but the goods are odd..."*
>
> An often cited phrase about Alaska men.

Architect

There are architects, but no architecture in Alaska. No one is willing to say this out loud, however, because architects are such sensitive souls.

Artist

Okay, we'll admit it. Artists are sexy. But, hey, does art ever pay? If you want to support a devoted mate in the land of the midnight sun, these guys are for you. How do you meet them? Art openings are great public events. Show up wearing something, well, rich. If a handsome Alaska artist asks what you do, just say you're independently wealthy. They'll flock. We guarantee it.

Attorney

The Alaska variety of this breed comes in two distinct types. The first is the corporate type, who is likely to work in one of the state's larger multi-named firms such as Huge and Thoughtless. If you like men in suits, go directly to Anchorage and find one of these. You'll probably have them all to yourself, since Alaska women are not all that impressed with this strain. The second variety professes to have more sensitive values and can be found struggling to make a living at a small or

> "The only difference between a guy in Anchorage and one in North Carolina is that the guy in Anchorage has a beard and a snowblower."
>
> Dillingham man on his competition.

20

independent law firm defending Alaskans' right to privacy and a permanent fund dividend check.

Author

Alaska authors are always on the verge of their big breakthrough. Ask him about his film option. Don't believe it.

Bureaucrat

Bureaucrats come in two distinct types, Juneau and Anchorage. The Juneau type professes to enjoy rain-soaked Southeast, likes to kayak in the fog, and is usually, in a word, moody. The Anchorage type is more of a go-getter, has a condo, and works at his job only to support his various sports addictions. (See also Jockaholic.)

Bush-Dweller

Longing for the romance of that little cabin in the woods? If so, these guys are for you. Identifiable by long hair and a beard, flannel shirt, bear tooth necklace, and heavy boots. These guys are rugged, and they'll expect you to be rugged too. Women are rated by these guys on a *"one bucket"* or *"two bucket"* basis: if you can carry two five gallon buckets of water at a time, you're in. So it might be worth

"Why dig an outhouse hole when you can tie a stick to two trees and move it every so often."

What a hunter trapper type told his soon-to-be ex-girl friend.

practicing this stunt at home. If you get good enough, you can enter the Wilderness Woman contest at the Talkeetna Bachelor Festival!

Bush Pilot

Often found in the bushes. An element of danger adds a veneer of glamour and sex appeal to the job of *"cab driver of the air."* Do you want to devote the rest of your life to supporting an airplane? Do you want an airplane in your living room for repairs? If your answer is yes, opportunities to travel and see the wilderness are unparalleled. However, this adventurous Alaska man is not for the woman prone to worrying, or air-sickness.

Carpenter

These come in union and nonunion varieties. Actually, almost every male in Alaska considers himself a carpenter. You can play this game too. If someone asks you if you can frame a house, just say sure. The truth is that some of the finest craftsmen in this profession find their way to Alaska, and if you're lucky, you'll see some of the fine Alaska home-building that is their trademark.

> "He thought he was handy because he lived around the corner, not because he could fix things."
>
> Ketchikan woman on an Alaska handyman.

Climber

Climbers live temporarily at the sea-level elevations of Alaska's more populated areas, while making enough money or the necessary arrangements to return to the heights where they truly feel at home and alive. If you are not prepared to go there with him, you won't be part of his *"real"* life. These guys are mostly broke. Expect to spend the rest of your life in a half-finished cabin with your clothes in cardboard boxes. (For exception see Doctors.)

Composer

The only one of these that we know of up here is a bit strange. Keeps his alarm clock in the refrigerator!

Construction Workers

These, too, come in union and nonunion types. The union variety gets paid more, but is likely to be unemployed for long periods of time. His life revolves around the archaic, complex, and nearly unfathomable union hiring rules. Prepare to listen patiently to discussions about the A-list, short calls, signing the book, business managers, and vesting. The nonunion construction worker lacks the same sense of brotherhood and team spirit.

> "If you really want to know about a guy, read what's on his hat."
>
> Former director of a woman's shelter.

Contractor

At one time, almost everyone in Alaska was a contractor. Those that hold on through the boom and bust cycles can be workaholics. Be sure to ask him if he has any hobbies. If he doesn't, he may work most of the time, in which case you should prepare to spend a lot of time by yourself.

Doctor

(See Climber)

Dog musher

Dog mushing is a fast paced, competitive, and monied sport these days. It used to be considered the macho sport, until they figured out that women are better mushers. The good mushers keep a kennel of fifty or more dogs, which isn't cheap. Caring for these dogs and taking them on training runs is a lot of work. No wonder the single guys are looking for a help-mate. Lots of opportunities to marry into a good team here! One woman we knew of spent two winters living with her dog musher beaux in a wall tent fifty miles (by dog-team of course) from Nenana. Don't say we didn't warn you.

> "Those women are too skinny. They look like bicycle frames."
>
> Musher on the Iditarod trail commenting about visiting Lower 48 women.

Engineer

Engineers are easy. In a scarce economy
of females, they find it hard to compete
with more macho-aggressive Alaska men,
so they are often more tolerant and
willing to accept you as you are, whether
you're overweight, or just weird. Most
engineers are stable, persistent, and
conventional. They may even support
you. To converse, you'll need to know
engineer-ese, so study up! Or just show
up with your lap-top, and tell them how
big your hard-drive is.

Entrepreneur

Warning! Danger! Watch Out!
(See also con man, liar, could-have-been,
should-have-been, would-have-been,
has-been, boomer, and loser.) (See also
unemployed.)

Environmentalist

Environmentalists are cute, homespun,
earthy, and usually from somewhere else.
They enjoy going to the wilderness in
their spare time. In Alaska, they are often
bureaucrats . (See also tree-hugger, sierra-
clubber)

"I keep ice cream in there during the winter."

Alaska man on why he keeps a file cabinet in his yard.

know your footwear
choose your type accordingly

Red Wings:
your basic work shoe
worn by those who
have a real job

Steel toed work shoes
aka CORKS:
worn by lumberjacks
and loggers

Red Tops
aka Juneau sneakers:
worn by state
workers and any
one else living in
southeast AK

inflate valve

Bunny Boots:
worn by dog
mushers, north
slope workers,
outdoors men,
construction
workers
keeps feet warm
at ~70°.

Leather Sneakers:
worn by tourists

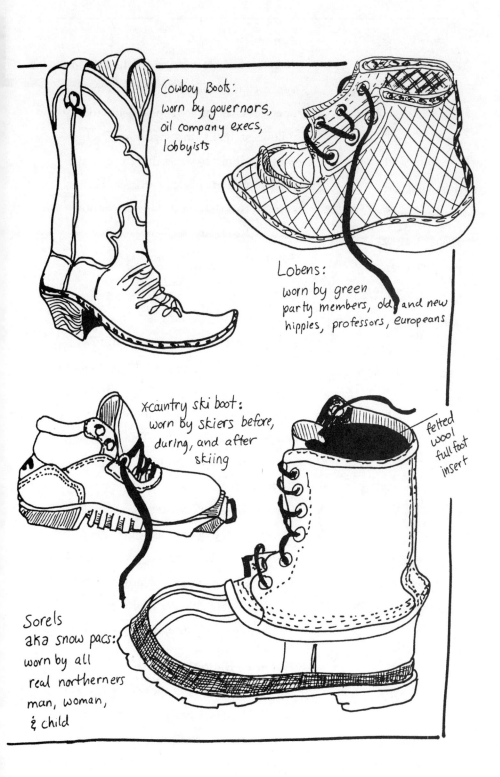

Cowboy Boots:
worn by governors,
oil company execs,
lobbyists

Lobens:
worn by green
party members, old and new
hippies, professors, europeans

x-country ski boot:
worn by skiers before,
during, and after
skiing

felted
wool
full foot
insert

Sorels
aka snow pacs:
worn by all
real northerners
man, woman,
& child

Explorer

"City bred Eastern dandies who seldom venture off the sidewalk without their knee-britches, dinky caps, pneumatic pillows, and silk underwear, and yet, earn headlines for trips that the average pioneer would consider no great hardship." (This definition courtesy of our favorite historian and University of Alaska professor Terrence Cole.)

Firefighter

Wilderness fire fighting is a time-honored occupation in Alaska. In the early 70s people would line up around the block in front of the state employment office to get hired for two weeks or a month during major fires. Now-a-days, things are more organized, and the professional firefighters work for the State Forestry Division, or for BLM. It's the ultimate seasonal job, day and night in the summer, with the winter off to go to Hawaii. The elite of the profession are the smoke jumpers: those who parachute out of airplanes directly into the fire zone.

Fisheries Biologist

Sounds scientific, but these people really spend the season camped out next to some remote stream counting fish at two hour intervals day and night. One little fishie...two little fishies...you get the idea.

Fishermen

Picture yourself carrying a load of brush on your back to your picturesque smokehouse on the banks of the Yukon, Nushagak or Kuskokwim River; or in the tiny galley of a fishing boat, cooking for the crew on a 24-hour halibut opening in rough weather, rolling on the high seas off Kodiak; or more probably, picture yourself at home with the kids while he's gone for weeks at a time during *"the season"* which can last from February til November. Good profit for a few high-rollers. Do you want to support a fishing boat for the rest of your life?

"When a woman gets off the plane the whole town knows."
Kodiak fisherman.

Fishermen come in several types, enumerated and defined here (by income level, of course). Want to meet them? Hang out on the docks at the small boat harbor in coastal towns such as Juneau, Valdez, Egigik, King Salmon, Naknek, Cordova, Dillingham, Wrangell, Homer, Seward, or Ketchikan. From the bottom of the totem pole to the top, it roughly goes like this:

Fisherman: **Deck hand**

Deck hands work on someone else's boat for a share (usually a smallish share) of the season's profits.

Fisherman: **Bow-picker**

Usually found in Southeast, they work a small open boat for salmon or halibut. Picture a 24-foot skiff with a two-hundred pound, five-foot-long halibut flopping in the bottom, staring with his one good eye.

Fisherman: **Hand troller**

Slightly higher in the pecking order, hand-trollers fish for salmon on multiple fishing lines from a relatively small boat. A romantic notion, but note that profit is limited. The multiple tall spruce poles that are rigged for lines on these boats are a dead giveaway.

Fisherman: **Set netter**

Set netters set gill nets just off shore, using a skiff from a set net site where they camp. This can be very profitable in Southwest Alaska areas like Dillingham, Nushagak, Eegigik, and King Salmon. But it is a lot of round-the-clock hard work during the relatively short season. At least they stay home off-season!

"My suggestion for an Alaska fragrance is, 'After Glow' ... the perfume that lingers when he doesn't."

Arizona woman on Alaska men.

Fisherman: **Gill netter**

Now we're getting into some serious income. Gill netters, or *"drifters"* set nets for salmon, working from smaller, picturesque wooden fishing boats, recognizable by the big hydraulic drum on the stern deck. Sometimes these are bow-pickers, with the drum on the bow deck. Gill netters spend most of their time and money fixing the boat and switching gear.

Fisherman: **Purse Seiner**

There is nothing quite as awesome as the purse seine fleet lined up in one of Alaska's small boat harbors. These are *"big money"* fishermen, so here's a little more detail. Using a good sized boat (50 feet and up) and lots of expensive gear, they string one end of a long net in the water from a special skiff which circles back to the boat. The bottom of the net is then drawn together with a drawstring like a purse, and the fish trapped in the *"purse"* are *"brailed"* into the hold of the boat with a dipper, or sucked up with a special vacuum. Look for large, newer boats, with the a tall perch for the lookout, a special hoist for nets, and extra wide and stubby aluminum skiffs on board. Want

> *"Women think these guys can change if only they have the love of a good woman ...it's a seductive myth."*
>
> Woman boarding the plane home.

to meet these guys? Get a job as a waitress at the "Reluctant Fisherman" in Cordova.

Fisherman: **Trawler**

We hate to admit that the trawlers fishing in the Bering Sea represent the biggest money of all. The reason we hate to admit it is that most of these boats are owned by Seattle-ites who hire some Alaskans, but generally speaking, most of this profit leaves the state. If you want a really rich Alaska fisherman, go to Seattle.

Fish Spotter

Yes, this is a job here in the north. It's the rodeo of aviation. Picture a cattle drive on the sea and in the air. Fish spotters flying in small planes look for schools of fish, then radio the info to the boat captains that have hired them. One spotter works for several boats. If you're invited as observer it's good to be part owl; your job will be to watch for other planes. Very dangerous, but big bucks.

Gold Miner

First-time-out gold miners are the epitome of the something-for-nothing, free money crowd. "You mean all that gold is out there and all I have to do is go dig it out?"

It sounds deceptively simple. Placer miners spend most of their time fixing their equipment. When the equipment is working, placer mining mostly involves moving dirt. Do you want to spend the rest of your life supporting a D-8, Grizzly, loader, dozer and various other yellow machines? Be sure to ask if he has ever made any money off his claim. If he shows you his gold in a glass vial, that's a pair of earrings; if he shows you the gold in five gallon buckets, we'd advise sticking around. But be careful, you may be the next victim of "gold fever."

Handyman

The Alaska handyman comes in two types, professional and amateur. A professional fixes things for a living. He would no more hire someone else to do home repairs than live in Southern California. But, does he want to spend his leisure time doing what he gets paid to do? No, he'd rather go hunting. The amateur handyman is innocent but dangerous. He does not make his living being handy, and therefore enjoys being handy in his spare time. His ultimate nirvana is buried in The Big Project.

> "She walked right by me without saying hello. That's the last time I fix her four wheeler."
>
> An Alaska handyman.

Beware: if the Big Project is ever actually finished, this guy is cast out from heaven. If a woman becomes involved in the Big Project, she risks becoming an Alaska Handyman divorce statistic.

Hippie, Old

Old hippies often support their antisocial lifestyle with stints as laborers on large development projects. With their long hair and distinctive ways, this type is often seen as strange by such fellow workers like the Pipeliners from Oklahoma.

Hippie, New

(See environmentalist.)

Laborer

The Laborers Union in Alaska can boast the highest percentage of members with advanced college degrees of any union in America. It's not unusual to find a Ph.D. raking asphalt or shoveling. Laboring is an honest profession in Alaska. Scratch a politician, lawyer, engineer, or doctor, and underneath you'll find a former member of Laborers Local #942. Bullshitting is an occupational hazard. These days being a card-carrying Laborer offers unchallenged proof that you are an Alaska man.

> "They use pickup trucks as lawn ornaments. The myth is that one day they'll get it running. Even the guys who never have and never will pick up a wrench collect these things."
>
> A Fairbanks neighbor.

M.C.P. (Male Chauvinist Pig)

Identifiable by his plaid flannel shirt, boots, baseball cap, and blue jeans worn fashionably low below the belly. Occasionally can be seen dressed up sporting a bolo tie with bear claw fastening. Often seen standing in a circle with others of his kind guffawing loudly at ribald jokes, dangling a cigarette from the corner of his mouth, and holding a can of beer in one hand while scratching his lower regions with the other. Listen for the M.C.P.'s mating call: "Wooowee, Baaaabbbeeeee!"

Mechanic

Also known as grease monkey. Every guy in Alaska considers himself a mechanic, as well as a carpenter. If you like mechanics, consider taking up auto-body painting, or getting a job as an auto parts delivery person. (They seem to only hire cute young blondes for this position.) Keep in mind that an unemployed mechanic may fix your car when it breaks down at 40 below; one with a job won't have time.

Nurse

There a number of the male varieties here in the north. They often double as mechanics or heavy equipment operators.

> "I would say if you want to get to know independent, interesting women go to Alaska."
>
> A visitor's observation.

a sampling of the species...

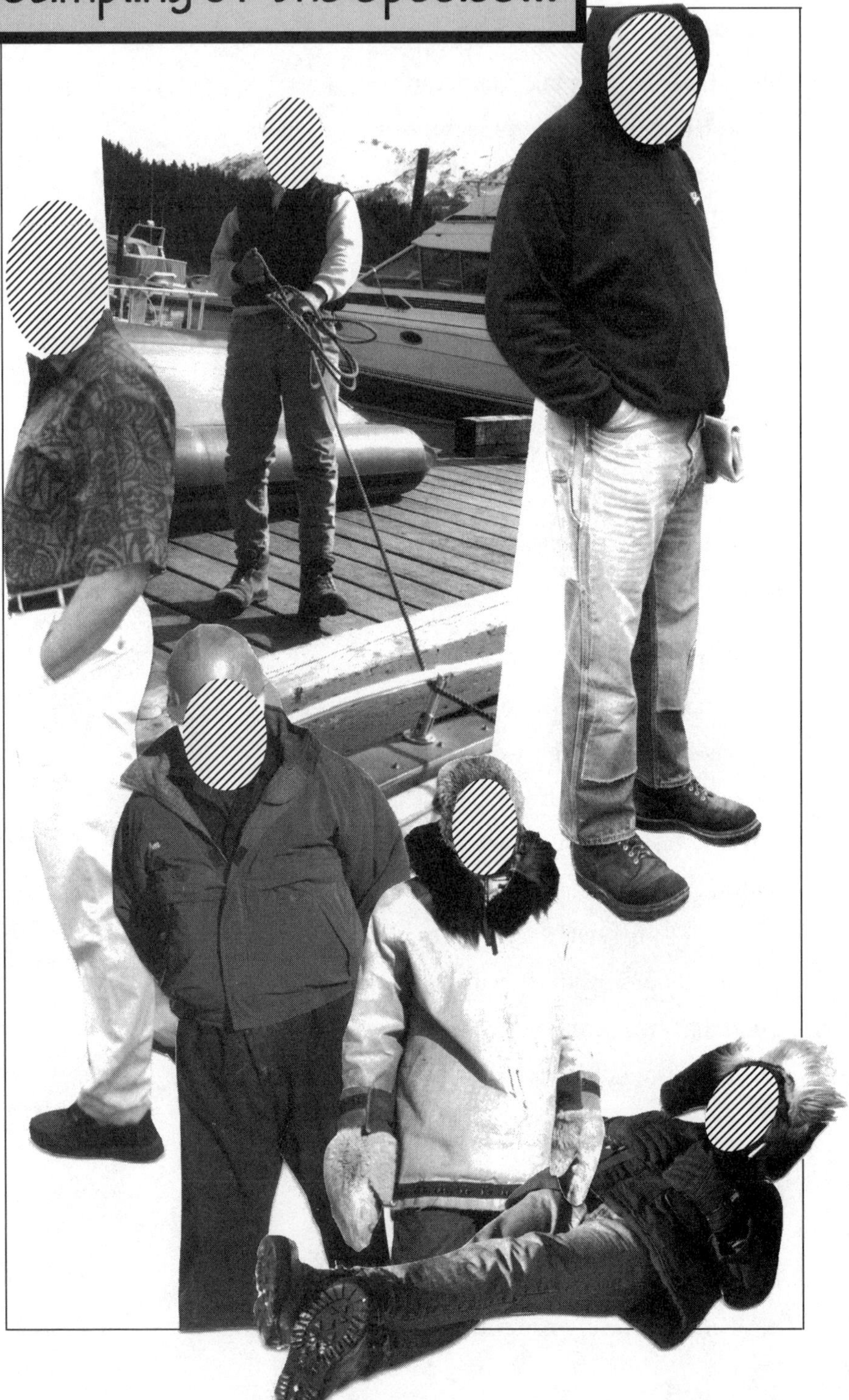

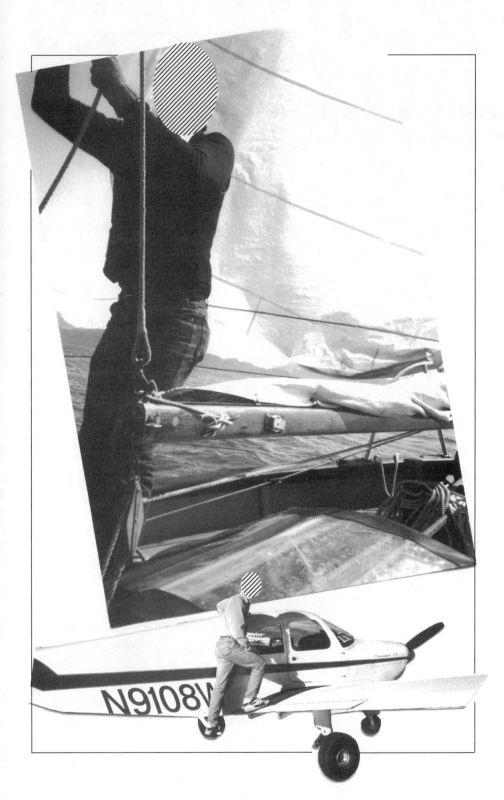

He could come in handy if you have a mishap in the wilderness.

Oil Field Worker

This is not really an Alaska lifestyle since most of these guys are from Texas and Oklahoma, where they return when not working.

Pipeliners

Also known as 798ers. These are the elite members of the pipeline welders union, Local 798, in Tulsa Oklahoma. They work all over the world on short jobs, wherever there's a high-pressure pipeline a-building. They mostly speak with a drawl, and a good many of them have forty acres and a mule somewheres in Bald Knob, Arkansas or Oak Grove, Louisiana. There are almost no women pipeliners, and no minorities, except for a few Oklahoma Indians, all of whom are called "Chief" by the other 798ers. Since they "boom-out" all over the world on a moment's notice, they are notoriously tough on wives. Few are on their first; a few are on their sixth, seventh, or even tenth sincere try at the institution of marriage.

"Do you know what an Alaska man's matching set of luggage consists of... two cardboard boxes sealed with duct tape."

An embarrassed mother.

Politician

There are three male varieties of this breed in Alaska: local, state, and national. The local strain is usually well meaning, has time on his hands, and is a masochist. The state variety also is usually well meaning, but is either more ambitious and can't find a job, or has no profession and likes to eat hors douvres. The national variety sold his soul long ago, likes airline travel, and is definitely committed to the adage out of sight, out of mind. In Alaska, our politicians are very accessible. Most people know the Governor, his cabinet members, and a dozen legislators by first name. If you find one of these guys to be particularly attractive, we'd encourage you to stride right up to him, call him by his first name, and ask him how the heck he's been doing. At the very least, he'll think he should know you and in the interest of being re-elected, will warmly grasp your hand and ask you to sit down for a chat.

> "I need a woman who knows paperwork. I could use some help to fill out my unemployment forms and permanent fund dividend application."
>
> Manley homesteader.

Professor

(See Howling Dog Saloon, Fairbanks.)

Rock and Roller

If the sun comes up at 2 am and sets at 12 am and you stay up 'til 5 am and sleep til after noon, which day is it? Alaska's rock and rollers are a very confused bunch in the summer, but they have a great time and truly appreciate women who truly appreciate their music.

Salesman

None of the hard-sell types survive in Alaska. Our independent streak simply will not tolerate it. So most of these guys are pretty low key and spend a lot of time chatting over cups of coffee. You can always spot an Outsider in this category; he's usually the regional sales manager from Seattle or Boise whose territory includes Alaska. He stands out like a sore thumb because his new cowboy boots, new blue jeans, highly polished leather belt and new flannel shirt are topped off with a too-slick haircut groomed with stiff mousse.

Scientist

Scientists live with their head in the Van-Allen belt, their feet firmly planted in glacier ice, and their eyes on their wallets. Scientific research in Alaska pays if you can play research institute politics, so if you're willing to host a run of cocktail parties for your beau and woo the well placed higher-ups he needs to impress, you may collect a specimen.

Sensitive '80s man

Usually a bureaucrat, or state worker, he doth protest that he really is a sensitive guy and all this jargon about Alaska MCP's, rednecks, and hippies slander his higher feelings.

Sensitive '90s man

The guy on the other end of the phone at Ron's Service Station in Fairbanks when it's been 40 degrees below zero for a week and your car won't start.

Snowbird

Here today, gone to Maui (as soon as the first dusting of snow hits the nearby mountains). This quasi-Alaska man returns faithfully every spring to begin the seasonal mating ritual at such pro-tected watering holes as the Howling Dog or Chilkoot Charlie's.

Student

Often looks like a caveman. Wears bunny boots and blue jeans with holes revealing

"I love being with Alaskan men. We've been lost in the air, we've drifted down rivers, we've almost had to eat our sled dogs... adventures never stop."
Female teacher in Fairbanks.

the long johns underneath. Carries 50 pounds of laundry in his backpack, lives in a pathetic cabin, hauls water in an old truck, makes $3000 in his senior year. Might make $30,000 after graduation. Pick up one of these guys at Hot Licks in Fairbanks or the Underground Bar in Anchorage while they're still cheap and get a real bargain.

Teacher

If you can find one that's single, he's got health benefits, dental coverage, and the summer off.

Trapper

Many go out a few days a year chasing furry critters through the woods. They spend the rest of their time in town setting their snares for you with stories about "the bear that almost ate me" or "the time I fell through the ice." (See also Bush-Dweller)

Used Car Salesman

The only one we ever heard of in Alaska is now married and selling real estate on Martha's Vineyard using his cell phone from the middle of his pool. This is another species that just doesn't survive long in the down-to-earth north country.

Wildlife Biologist

Spends most of his summer in the *"field"* chasing, counting or otherwise bothering caribou, wolves, foxes, rabbits or what have you. Much easier to find in the winter months in state or federal office buildings, where they are often glued to their desks arguing with other wildlife biologists over data and daydreaming of next summer's fieldwork. The easiest way to meet one is to wander into either the Alaska Environmental Center in Anchorage or the Northern Alaska Environmental Center in Fairbanks.

Zoologist

What are they? What do they really do? Let us know if you know.

"When she came to visit I gave her one drawer in the file cabinet and two drawers in the bureau. After all, a woman needs a place for her stuff."

Alaska man on understanding women.

It may look disorganized
to you, but he knows
where everything is.

Think of it as his office, where great entrepreneurial ideas are spawned. There may be a market niche for a coin operated wringer washing machine. Faith Popcorn, what do you think?

Floatplane Pond
Iditarod Checkpoint
Smokejumpers Bunkhouse
Public Hearing on Subsistence
Carpenters Union Hall
Oil Spill Clean-up Station
Public Hearing on Offshore Drilling
Open North American Sled Dog Race
July Fourth Parade
Gold Bearing Creeks
Bun on the Run
State Courthouse
Mussel Farm
Fish Camp

The Meet Of The Matter

Global Warming Research Plot • The Docks • Firewood Cutting Permits • Bush Airport Waiting Room • Public Hearing on Forest Development • Ice Festival • Yukon Quest Sled Dog Race • Laborers Union Hall • Small Plane Tie Downs • Public Showers • Miners Ball • University

CHAPTER 3

meeting the Alaska man

Where to go, when to go, what to see, what to do, and most important, who you're likely to meet where and when.

Picturesque Southeast Alaska, with high snowcapped peaks and the protected inland passage waters dotted with thousands of forested islands, is home to hundreds of rugged fishermen, loggers and foresters. Alaska's capital city, Juneau, is populated by numerous well-paid state workers, legislators, and bureaucrats, for those of you who like men in ties.

At the opposite end of the men's-wear spectrum is Alaska's remote southwest region, where we don't know if you'll ever see a tie. Southwest includes Bristol Bay (the home of high stakes salmon fishing in the summer), the exotic Aleutian chain, and the Yukon Kuskokwim Delta, home of the Yupik Eskimos.

Alaska's Southcentral Region is dominated by Anchorage, the largest city in the state. What kind of men live here? All kinds.

Unlike anywhere else Alaska, Anchorage features an urban environment much like cities in the rest of the U.S. But the best thing about Los Anchorage, as it's known by the rest of the state's residents, is that it's so close to Alaska! Hiking, mountaineering, and skiing are available within the city limits. Close by is the Kenai Peninsula, Anchorage's playground and home of the trophy-size King Salmon (a great place to connect with all those sport fishermen.)

Want to really get away from it all? Try Alaska's Northern region. The highest per capita population of males is in the transient outpost of Prudhoe Bay, the center of Alaska's North Slope oil fields. But to see another side of the Arctic, travel to Kotzebue, Nome, Barrow, the Inupiat Eskimo villages, or to Anaktuvak Pass in the awe inspiring Brooks Range.

Finally, and our bias is showing, the great Interior, gateway to the last frontier and the real spirit and heart of Alaska. This is the spot for those of you who like really great summer weather, a really long dog mushing season, and perfect cross-country skiing for almost eight months. Many Interior Alaskans actually swear that Fairbanks has the world's most perfect climate. (Many Anchorage residents swear that Fairbanks residents are simply nuts.) You can imagine what kind of guys live in the Interior: skiers, hockey players, dog mushers, ice fishermen, gold miners, musicians, handymen, scientists, and a few writers who enjoy winter solitude.

When to Come

What's the best time for a visit? Well, summer is glorious.

The sun is up 22 hours a day all summer and everyone is moving double-time. There are lots of things to get done before winter, the building season is short, and there are only twelve summer weekends to squeeze in all those river trips! Summer is the time for wilderness raft, canoe, and hiking adventures, and for fishing, which guarantees a high concentration of males along Alaska's rivers and streams.

Want to really get noticed? Show up midwinter. Believe it or not, mid-February through March features great winter weather. You get sunny days, romantic moonlit nights, undulating northern lights, plus all those dog races. Along with the well known Iditarod, starting in Anchorage and ending in Nome, the Yukon Quest race from Fairbanks to Whitehorse, the North American Championship Dog Sled Races in Fairbanks, and the Fur Rendez-vous in Anchorage occur February through April. Or come in November or December during the holiday season.

Alaskans, single and married alike, are famous for their warm hospitality. We love to pass this warmth along. You'd have to be quite unpleasant *not* to wind up with a heartfelt invitation to holiday gatherings at this time of year. During the winter the seasonally employed have time to visit and play, and many guys from the bush or smaller communities come into town to visit and to do their shopping. It's a great time to come and get to know Alaskans. Everyone was new once.

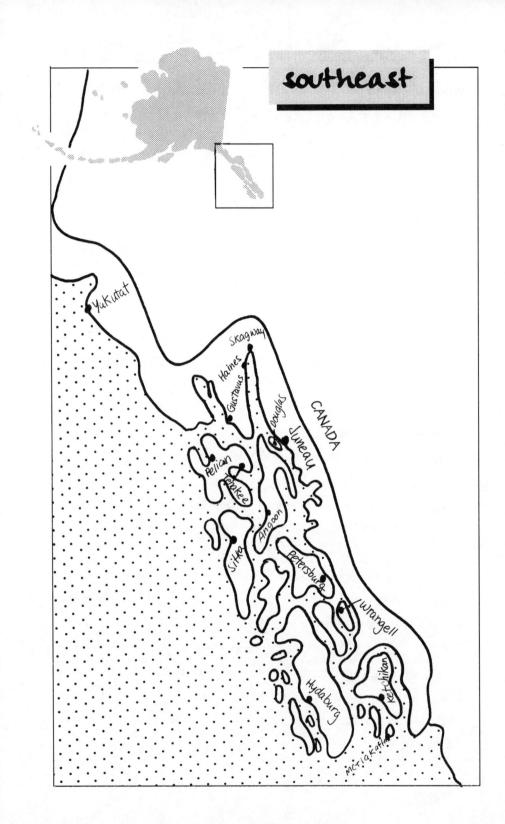

southeast

Yukutat

Skagway

Haines

Gustavus

Douglas

Juneau

CANADA

Pelican

Tenakee

Angoon

Sitka

Petersburg

Wrangell

Hydaburg

Ketchikan

Metlakatla

SOUTHEAST ALASKA

Southeast is gorgeous. The meeting of mountains, glaciers, and the protected waters of the inland passage make for some truly speechless moments. Of course it does rain a lot... The towns in Southeast are only accessible by ferry or air. The Alaska Marine Highway ferries are a great meeting place in and of themselves. The trip from Bellingham, Washington to Haines is a fabulous introduction to the state: a three-day Alaskan-style party. Don't bother with a stateroom, just sleep out in the solarium with the locals. Bring a tent for privacy. If you don't have a car, you can usually walk onto the ferries without reservations any time of year except the summer months. It's a great freewheeling way to travel. We recommend it highly, if you hadn't noticed. A cruise may be a fine way to see the sights in deluxe comfort, but you won't meet any Alaskans.

Juneau

Juneau is a wonderful place, if you like bureaucrats. Actually it's small and quaint enough to be charming, but sophisticated enough not to be small-minded. All wrapped up in an exquisite setting, the state capital is, from January to May, home to Alaska's legislators and their innumerable young and eager aides. In the summer months, down-town is taken over by cruise ship passengers, not a local to be found. Year round you'll find state workers (environmentalists and fishermen) with a back-to-the-land-and-water mentality combined with a safe state job. If you like folkies too, come in April for the Juneau Folk Festival.

• *The Red Dog Saloon* is a classic. It's where the locals go to find the tourists. Not a bad place to position yourself if you're looking to get met. Just wear a matching outfit so they'll know you're new in town!

bachelor cabin in the southeast

50 gallon drums -
the ever present fixture in
the north, you never know
when you might need one

scaffolding - an always
present feature of
an out-of-pocket
building project

90lb building felt tar paper
covers the outside until he
saves enough for siding

Alaska man
at work

crabpots
stored for
a friend who
recently married

entry - wooden board
with slats until he has
time to make stairs

bathtub will be
installed when he
has time to dig a
well and install the
indoor plumbing

old girlfriend
is storing
her things
on his land
until she
gets her
own place

wooden boardwalk to the beach, easy
access to the boat to go fishing

• *Heritage Coffee House* is a good stop for a latte pick-me-up in the morning or an afternoon cheesecake break. This is the exclusive hangout of Juneau's ultra-too-cool population .

• *The Triangle* is situated strategically at the corner of Franklin and Main; this watering hole allows you to really scope out the locals. Sit down at the bar for a bratwurst and a beer and watch all of Juneau pass by through the one-way-glass picture window; that is, *if* you can squeeze in between the regulars.

• *The Channel Bowl* where locals hang out. It has the best chicken salad in the state. High powered state officials wander in for break-fast or lunch, check their hot air at the door, and enjoy the fun atmo-sphere created by the wise-cracking owners and servers.

• *The Alaska Hotel* go here and tell them it's your birthday. They'll insist you take a birthday soak in the downstairs hot tub. The sign says no bubble bath. Ignore it.

• *The Armadillo* is not to be missed for great Tex-Mex and a friendly atmosphere. Savvy locals come here for the best nachos and chili in Southeast Alaska. Maybe the easiest place in town to strike up a conversation with that Juneau-ite you spotted dancing the night before at one of the night spots on Franklin Street.

• *The Fiddlehead Restaurant* has fabulous food and is the best place to plug into the New Age crowd. This is also a favorite with intellectuals who reappear on Sunday mornings with *New York Times* in hand. Regardless of the ambiance, we have to say that these folks dish out some of the best and healthiest food in the state.

• *The Silver Bow Inn* is a charming, antique-filled, former bakery, now restored. During the legislative session, you'll see Alaska's movers and shakers lobbying each other for all kinds of things over breakfast, lunch and dinner.

• At *Luna's* it's the yuppie legislative set and the who's who of Alaska lunch. Arrive early if you think you might be interested in bumping into them..

• *Baranof Hotel* is the place to wander into for a real political education during the legislative session. Alaska deals, like the pipeline agreements, the permanent fund , and the abolishment of state income tax, have been cut in this historic hotel since the early thirties. If you're dreaming of someone with money, put on your cocktail dress, honey, and look for an oil lobbyist.

• Stroll around on the docks at the small boat harbors at Auke Bay and Aurora. The scenery is exquisite and quite a few single Alaska men make their homes on their boats in these harbors.

• Hike the trail up Mt. Roberts or head out to Silverbow Basin, a fabulous mountain valley just a short walk out of town. We can't guarantee you'd meet anybody, but they'd be nice if you did. In any case, it's a great hike, you'll look healthy.

Douglas

Douglas, a wonderful little town across the channel from Juneau proper, has a character and hang-outs all its own.

• *Louie's* is the place if you've targeted the large-biceped commercial fisherman type, you'll likely find him here at night. Wander in, order a beer, and after a while put your quarter on the pool table. If you've dressed blue collar, then it shouldn't be long before you find yourself with a handsome opponent.

• The beach at the Northern end of Douglas Island is a great place to catch a softball game, have a barbecue, and feast your eyes on some outstanding scenery. Great for bird and wildlife viewing too.

Tenakee

Tenakee hot springs is a great place for anything to happen. It's pretty small though, so you might want to bring your entertainment with you. In fact, you have to take a boat or the ferry to get there, so maybe you'll meet some commercial fishermen, or a yacht owner who's touring Southeast.

Sitka

Sitka is a fabulously scenic town with a colorful Russian heritage. Go in June for the culture crowd at the summer music festival. Or try the writer's symposium in the spring. Sitka is where Michener stationed himself while writing his mega novel *Alaska*.

• The Alaska Loggers Association convention in June is a real must if you're after the classic lumberjack type. If it happens to coincide with a herring opening that gets canceled, you're in for the time of your life.

• *The Pioneer Bar* is really classic, complete with a world-class collection of fishing boat photographs. It's a great place to catch the locals.

• *Shee Atika Hotel* for some sophisticated swank, where you might catch some deals in progress between the corporate types.

• The *Channel Club* is recommended for dinner steaks, seafood, and the best salad bar in the state. This is a real insider's tip, because you'd never know by looking that this joint has the best food in town; we can guarantee you'll meet locals here.

Petersburg

Home of Norwegian bachelor fishermen, cousins of the Norwegian bachelor farmers. Don't miss the Little Norway Festival, another classic Alaska small town street party, flavored with Lutefisk. If you happen to have a little Norwegian heritage in your family tree, you'll be welcomed like family and looked over as bride material for sure.

Wrangell

Loggers and fishermen, are here, with a few misplaced back-to-the-landers thrown in to shake things up a bit. Wrangell is set in a corner of the majestic rain forest with the best weather in Southeast. The docks in the small boat harbor are the place to hang out. Be sure to visit *Chief Shakes House*. If you've followed our advice and taken the ferry trip, you'll be greeted by the children of Wrangell selling natural garnets from a nearby formation. Garnets bring good luck in love, so by all means, buy a few and keep them in your pocket.

Ketchikan

Ketchikan, the first Alaska town if you're traveling north by the ferry, is the second largest town in Southeast. A town of fishermen and fishermen's bars and rain. Will its working waterfront survive the influx of yuppies looking for that authentic experience? Like many Southeast coastal communtiies, Ketchikan becomes overrun with tourists and cruise ship traffic during the summer, and locals tend to make themselves scarce. Don't miss *Dolly's House*, on the scenic Creek Street boardwalk, a tourist attraction, but a classic one, and a kind of a shrine to a classic Alaska woman.

Haines

A surprise at the beginning of the road system, an artists' colony.
Loggers and fishermen live here too, and people who want to get
away from it all in a civilized small town. Camp out at Loutek Inlet,
or stay at the *Halsingland Hotel,* the former officers quarters of historic
Ft. Seward. Ask for a room with one of those old, enormous claw
footed bathtubs, and dream about a handsome army officer guarding
a pioneer outpost at the turn of the century.

Skagway

Skagway was the jumping off place for the Klondike Goldrush. The
downtown has been restored (or taken over, depending on your point
of view) by the National Park Service. It is a wonderful place to visit
and soak up gold rush heritage. It's now the jumping off place for
hikers on the *Chilkoot Pass Historic Trail.* The place is positively
overrun with tourists during the summer.

Gustavus

The jumping off point for Glacier Bay, Gustavas is another teeny get-
away town in Southeast. On the shores of Icy Strait, not far from the
Pacific Ocean, it's surrounded by snow capped peaks. This might
be the place to indulge in that guided sea-kayaking trip you've been
thinking of. Good place to meet a yuppie setting-up a bed &
breakfast.

"Everyone
in Alaska
is running
from
something."

Social worker in
Anchorage.

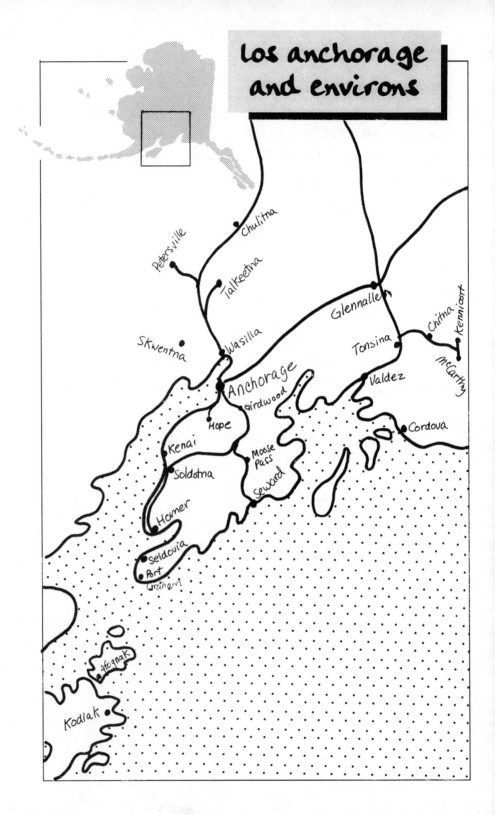

los anchorage
and environs

Chulitna

Petersville

Talkeetna

Glennallen

Chitina

Kennicott

Skwentna

Wasilla

Tonsina

McCarthy

Anchorage

Girdwood

Valdez

Hope

Cordova

Kenai

Moose
Pass

Soldotna

Seward

Homer

Seldovia

Port
Graham

Afognak

Kodiak

SOUTHCENTRAL ALASKA

Southcentral Alaska includes Anchorage, the Kenai Peninsula, and Prince William Sound. In between is the Matanuska-Susitna Valley, a magnificent and varied area the size of West Virginia, with mountains, glaciers, farming communities and more. Also on the road system in Southcentral is Wrangel-St. Elias National Park. Here there are fewer tourists, and lots of Alaska men who are climbing, biking hiking, mining, fishing, and generally proving how tough they are. The Kenai Peninsula is Anchorage's playground, summer and winter. Catching a magnificent Kenai River king salmon is every Alaska Man's dream, and they flock here in all shapes and sizes (the men, that is).

Anchorage

Where else could you find an authentic Korean barbecue named after the American soap opera, *Falcon Crest*. The state's largest city is still no major metropolitan area by anyone's standards. It's home to a diverse population of about 250,000 including lawyers, state agency employees, federal agency employees, lawyers, boomers, libertarians, more lawyers, and an endless supply of the seemingly sensitive New Age '90s kind of guys (the ones who wish they'd gone out and built a cabin in the woods and trapped for the winter, but just haven't gotten around to it yet). Frankly, the best thing about Anchorage itself is that you sure can get to a lot of great places for the weekend from there. But while you're in town, here are the spots you'll want to frequent, depending of course, on the type of guy you want to meet. (Once you're in Alaska you can find your way to the local yellow pages, where each of these establishments proudly lists their address).

• *Chilkoot Charlie's* attracts the scruffy blue jean and biker crowd. If you really want to get attention here go into the ladies' room, where a graphic on the wall sports a toilet seat that appears to cover Charlie's privates. While you're waiting in line, lift up the seat. As soon as you do, a very loud buzzer will sound in the bar, and you'll emerge from the ladies' room to loud cheers and guffaws.

• *Club Paris* looks like those dark, atmospheric restaurants that your parents took you to in the '50s and '60s; candles on the tables, thick rich cuts of prime rib, salami and black olive hors d'oeuvres. You get the picture. *Club Paris* is still happily spinning in this time warp, and we Alaskans love it. You'll find all ages, shapes and sizes here, meshing well, chatting each other up.

• *Cyrano's* the downtown bookstore and espresso hangout for the literary set. The perfect place to browse the poetry section and catch someone's eye.

• *Downtown Deli* is owned by a former Anchorage mayor, now governor, and his partners. Whether or not Tony is in there pouring coffee, this tends to be a hangout for local politicos. With real corned beef and pastrami sandwiches, blintzes, and chicken soup, the place attracts refugee lawyers and doctors from the east coast.

• *F Street Station* boasts standing room only most Friday nights. Who's there? Young, upwardly mobile professionals who make those outrageous salaries, but have that special Alaska scent, *Eau de Jock*.

• *Fly-By-Night Club* is where you'll find Mr. Whitekeys. There's outrageous humor with a generous helping of spam jokes. Hit this club sometime between June 1 and September 15 during the annual run of "The Whale Fat Follies." Make your reservations at least six weeks in advance and when you do, ask for a table front and center. Then, if you're lucky (read: laugh heartily and often at Mr. Whitekeys' jokes), he may just pick you to hold the oosik under the spotlight during one of the shticks near the end of the show. The rest is up to you!

• *Great Alaska Bush Company* by all means, avoid this joint. It's strictly for 1960's style male bonding. The men you will meet here will be small minded and ugly.

• *Hogg Brothers Cafe* is the last great home of the greasy spoon. Make the breakfast scene here on a weekend morning. Bring a book with a conversation-provoking cover and cozy up to the counter next to a blond, mustachioed runner who comes in to pore over the *Daily News* while eating his weekly quota of grilled whatever. Like most Alaskans, he seeks balance in his life.

• *Gwennie's* is where the big and tall Alaska men hang out - lots of those oversize belt buckles. Great Alaska atmosphere. Best for breakfast, but be sure to starve yourself for two or three days ahead of time so you can keep up.

• *Merrill Air Field* is located in the center of town. If you want to meet a basic bush pilot this is the place. Head on down to the FAA station at Merrill Field then hitch a ride to Fairbanks or anywhere. Of course, the longer the ride, the more time you'll have to get to know the pilot. Be sure to sit in the copilot's seat; it will more than likely be offered to you, if he knows you're from out of town and you look the least bit excited about "being in my first Cessna!" Or for safer exposure, try *Peggy's Airport Cafe* across the street and meet the pilots over a very healthy slice of pie.

• *Regal Alaska Hotel* overlooks the Lake Hood float plane pond. On summer afternoons at 5:00 lawyers, politicians, power brokers, entrepreneurs and dilettantes are on the terrace. This place really hops during a power outage; it's the only bar in town with an emergency generator.

• *Saks* is a favorite with one of the authors, but not because of its Alaska flavor. This gourmet coffee house could be anywhere in the Pacific Northwest, as could the yuppies and artistic types who frequent it. Great curried banana soup and pasta dishes.

• *Simon and Seafort's* is for lawyers and yuppies, has terrific views of migrating beluga whales, as well as a yard-long list of beers and the best collection of rare and vintage scotches on the West Coast.

South of Anchorage

Leave the urban scene behind and drive south to the less civilized corners of the Municipality.

Turnagain Arm scenery has been likened to the Norwegian Fjords, but don't be distracted, there are some important hunting prospects in this region. If you're into rock climbing, you might want to try a rappelling date off the rock cliffs between Anchorage and Girdwood. It always looks like great fun. Watch the wind surfers found just off shore who taunt death with wind surfing runs down the waters of Turnagain Arm, defying the strongest tides in the Western Hemisphere. A word of caution - don't go on the mud flats; they're dangerous!

Girdwood

If they are into downhill skiing, doctors, lawyers, and dentists have their second to fourth homes here. Girdwood is home of *Alyeska Ski Resort*. Dress for skiing, or actually do it, at Alyeska anytime from

what he wears

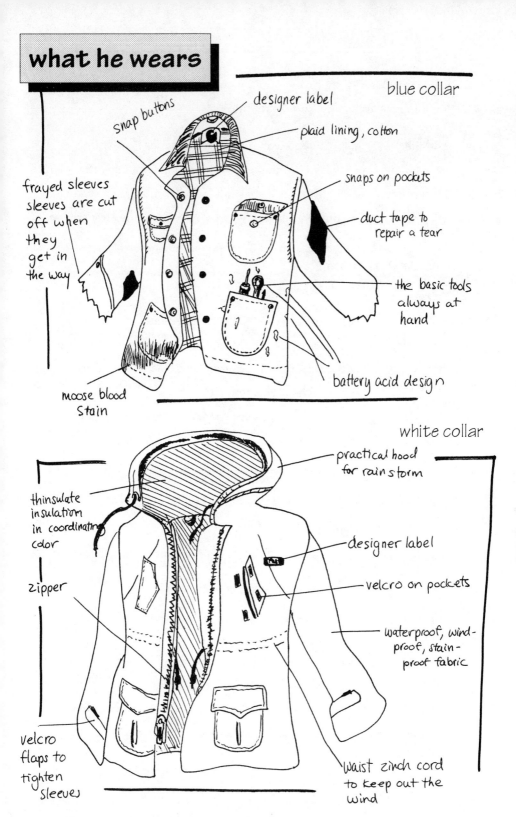

blue collar

snap buttons

designer label

plaid lining, cotton

snaps on pockets

duct tape to repair a tear

frayed sleeves sleeves are cut off when they get in the way

the basic tools always at hand

moose blood stain

battery acid design

white collar

practical hood for rainstorm

thinsulate insulation in coordinating color

designer label

velcro on pockets

zipper

waterproof, windproof, stainproof fabric

velcro flaps to tighten sleeves

waist zinch cord to keep out the wind

October to May. Either way, you'll meet lots of attractive men in the bar and probably enjoy some good music.

• While you're in Girdwood, eat at the *Double Muskie Restaurant* for fabulous Cajun food. You have to wait so long for a table that you invariably make all kinds of new friends before you've been seated. Or, just order the gumbo at the bar while you soak up the atmosphere.

North of Anchorage

Talkeetna

This is the home of the original *Alaska Bachelor Festival.* Need we say more? These guys are crazy. In the spring and summer, Talkeetna is the center of activity for the climbing crowd, Mt. McKinley climbers in particular. Your chances of meeting attractive, single climbers from all over the world are high; your chances of distracting them from their peak quest are low.

• *Talkeetna General Store* is a good place to strike up a conversation. Do it in a low key manner, and you may be lucky enough to get invited to an evening fish fry on the river.

• The bar at the *Fairview Inn* is the traditional watering hole for many locals.

Hatcher Pass

Fourteen miles from Wasilla, but looks like the Alps. Check out the food at the *Hatcher Pass Lodge,* or the bar scene at the *Motherlode Lodge.* This area offers great hiking and great cross country skiing in the winter, and who knows who you'll meet at the top.

KENAI PENINSULA

Hope

Make a right turn off the highway for a visit to Hope, the little log cabin town where a bunch of lonely bachelor miners first advertised for brides in 1985 and set off the current Alaska Bachelor phenomenon.

Moose Pass

The turn-off to Seward will take you through Moose Pass. Stop in at the *Moose Pass Roadhouse* and *Estes Brothers Store* for a glimpse of Alaska the way it used to be and a chance meeting with the Alaska truck drivers that may be passing through.

Seward

Seward has a great fourth of July celebration, including a grueling foot race straight up Mt. Marathon. A great street party and a great place to meet Alaska men.

• A stroll down the docks may yield a few interesting conversations.

• Better yet, if you can handle yourself really well in a kayak, rent one of these tumblers, put in at the boat dock, and watch a million handsome fishermen come to your rescue when you capsize "unintentionally."

• A cruise through the Kenai Fjords National Park will give you lots to talk about later at the bars. Or, hike to nearby Exit Glacier or Lost Lake.

Kenai River

Fishing and boating the Kenai River, from Cooper Landing to Kenai, attracts men throughout the summer. Check with the Alaska Department of Fish and Game to get the dates of the salmon seasons and plan to be there. Be sure to buy an Alaska fishing license, and set yourself up with some cheap fishing gear. Then all you'll need to do is walk down the river bank, where the fishermen are lined up shoulder to shoulder. Elbow your way in next to the most attractive prospect, and cast away! Signing on with a guided fishing trip, or renting a canoe are other options.

Soldotna

Stop at *Ken's Alaskan Tackle* in Soldotna. You can't miss the 23-foot spawned-out Humpie on the roof. Hang out by the fishing gear and ask the guys for advice.

Homer

Homer, at the end of the road on the Kenai Peninsula, might be the hippest place in Alaska, but there's a bad ratio here (more women than men.) Author and storyteller Tom Bodett might leave the light on for you; he surely has lots of buddies he'd be glad to fix you up with, if it would make a good story. (*Don't* tell him we sent you!) Or mingle with the generation Xer's camping out on the spit. A classic Alaska hangout.

• Fish, watch fishermen deliver their catch to the canneries, and check out the boats at the small boat harbor. Some fishermen are always there working on their gear.

• Go out on a halibut charter to catch one of the big ones! You'll feel just like the macho guys and be the talk of the docks, too.

•*The Salty Dog Saloon* on the Homer Spit is definitely worth a visit. Home of the old salts, do some man-watching here.

• *Lands End Resort* offers the most breathtaking view of scenic Kachemak Bay. Note the guy with the laptop computer, sitting by the window. He's a tourist posing as a writer, trying to meet women.

• *Alice's Champagne Palace* in downtown Homer is where things really get hopping after 10, with all the Anchorage yuppies down for the weekend, plus the locals, and the best dance band in town. Don't overlook the band members!

• *Smoky Bay Coop* sports the likeness of Dobie Gillis and Meynard G. Krebs with time to ponder.

• *McDonalds* for morning coffee is where some of the more crusty and colorful locals make their plans for the day. Listen to the conversation, and casually interrupt to ask their advice on your own plans. Before you know it you'll have an invitation to help him work on his plane or clean fish.

• *Two Sisters* is a small coffee shop in the old part of town next to the Bunnel Street Gallery (great art stop). Good eats, good place to regroup and trade tales with other women, and because of the female bonding, the men stop in to check out the scene.

• *Boat Yard Cafe* is a good place to visit just before the fishing season starts, generally May through June. It's located in the boat yard, where the men are prepping their boats or looking for work. There's good odds here. One of us was there on a Thursday afternoon, it was sixteen men to one woman. But keep in mind that old Alaska adage, the odds are good, but the goods are odd.

• Don't forget to wander through the actual boat yard. To make a good impression, tell him you're handy with a sander and you've won prizes for your macramé knots.

FEMALE
Roommate
——WANTED——

Adult male with unfinished 2-bedroom house and big pile of dirty dishes looking for roommate...

▼ $200/month + most of housework (I hate dishes)

▼ ALSO, I will trade out 1st month's rent for light carpentry & painting help, and up to ½ of future months' rent for help with other projects, as needed. Experience not necessary, just willing to learn.

▼ Must be over 18

▼ Pets... maybe

▼ straight or lesbian unimportant (I won't bother your girlfriends if you don't bother mine)

NON-SMOKING HOUSE • ON BIKE PATH • VOLLEYBALL NET

WASHER & DRYER — AND RUSTY FAIRBANKS WATER

Need motivated roommate to inspire me to finish building this house

 leave message on machine

Want ad found by the authors on a bulletin board in Fairbanks. Is this a statement on Fairbanks or on the man?

Seldovia

A romantically scenic little town across Kachemak Bay from Homer, accessible by ferry or charter boat. July fourth is the big weekend here. A good place to meet log rollers, ax thowers, and canoe jousters.

Kodiak Island

Flying over this island may remind you of another emerald isle, depending on your ancestry. Kodiak is accessible via ferry from Homer or Seward, or from Homer by air. Go in August for the outdoor plays and the salmon derby, and for the really wild fishermen, reputedly the state's wildest. You'll find them in the local bars. Kodiak may have the highest number of bars per capita in the state, or does it just seem that way?

VALDEZ / CORDOVA / WRANGEL-ST. ELIAS NATIONAL PARK

Northeast from Anchorage via the scenic Glenn and Richardson highways, four major mountain ranges meet in Wrangell St. Elias National Park. This park has 9 of the 16 highest mountain peaks and the largest number of ice fields of any national park in the United States, plus scenery to rival the Swiss Alps.

Chitna

Chitna must be mentioned as the site of a red-salmon dip-net fishery on the Copper River. It attracts men from Fairbanks and Anchorage in June and July. Watch them brave the sweeping current of the mighty river with nets attacted to 25-foot-long poles.

McCarthy

McCarthy, everyone's favorite funky, semi-inhabited ghost town, is the gateway to Kennicott. Mountain biking, which increases in popularity every year. Lots of lycra found here.

• The bar at the *McCarthy Lodge* is a classic. You can stay at the lodge, or pitch your tent out back and take your meals and showers at the lodge. Don't forget your mountain bike.

• Five miles beyond, the main attraction is the abandoned *Kennicott Copper Mine* which hangs on the side of a dramatic mountain overlooking a magnificent glacier. Hike or explore the ruins.

• Then stop in at the *Kennicott Glacier Lodge,* order an Alaskan Amber on the deck and contemplate.

Valdez

Accessible by road, about eight hours from Anchorage. One of the world's great drives will take you through scenic Thompson Pass to Valdez, which is located on gorgeous Prince William Sound, home of the now infamous Exxon Valdez oil spill. This town will have major traffic in environmental specialists and government officials for years to come. But, by the time you get there, the town's tourism opportunities will have recovered, and maybe even its sense of humor.

• Be sure to take a fabulous fishing trip. Don't forget to get a picture of yourself with a trophy halibut to impress the guys.

• Take a tour with *Stan Stephen's Charters.* Ask Stan for the real story of the Exxon Valdez oil spill.

• Be sure and visit *The Pipeline Club* where Joseph Hazelwood is said to have had those last fateful drinks.

• Come in the winter for the "Extreme Ski Competition" and the growing winter sports scene, including glacier snow boarding and heli-skiing.

Cordova

Cordova is a colorful, little town with an eclectic population, and it is accessible by ferry from Valdez or Whittier. But to get right to the point, the high rollers in town are the purse seine fishermen.

• Stroll the docks while you check out all the boats with their colorful fishing gear.

• *The Reluctant Fisherman* during the season, has a nice little tavern. Locals and tourists alike hang out here. It's a pretty fair place to acclimatize, read, slow down. And of course, there's always the locals' table for morning coffee in the coffee shop.

• Drive out to the Copper River and see the Million Dollar Bridge, a part of the Copper River Railroad that was the Pipeline of its time. (For a real feeling for the era, and a historical look at Alaska Macho Man, read *The Iron Trail*, by Rex Beach.)

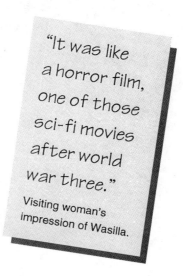

"It was like a horror film, one of those sci-fi movies after world war three."
Visiting woman's impression of Wasilla.

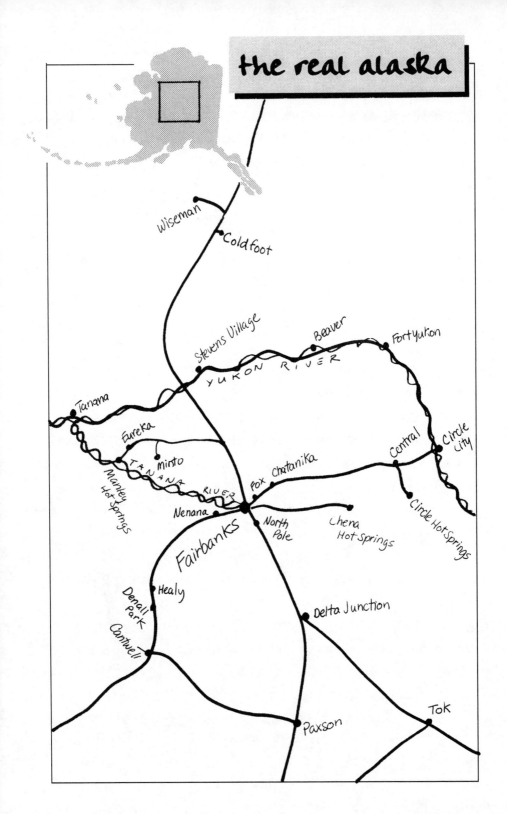

the real alaska

Wiseman
Coldfoot
Stevens Village
Beaver
Fort Yukon
YUKON RIVER
Tanana
Eureka
Minto
TANANA
RIVER
Fox
Chatanika
Central
Circle City
Manley Hot Springs
Nenana
North Pole
Chena Hot Springs
Circle Hot Springs
Fairbanks
Healy
Denali Park
Delta Junction
Cantwell
Paxson
Tok

INTERIOR ALASKA

Interior Alaska is a vast region covered with spruce and birch forests. The wide flat valleys of the Yukon and Tanana Rivers create a home for many species of wildlife and breeding ground for migrating waterfowl. Many native Athabaskan Indian villages are located on the banks of the rivers. Summers, late May til early August, are a daily twenty-four hour riot of intensity; the sun never sets. The weather is clear, hot, and sunny, with temperatures in the 80's and sometimes 90's. Bring your short shorts and prepare for volleyball, but don't forget the mosquito dope. Fall usually begins with rain in mid August. Leaves start to change in late August, and Indian summer, a yellow-orange color fest of clear fall weather arrives in September, a great time for hiking, biking, and Denali National Park without tourists. Dog mushing and cross-country skiing begin in October and might last til mid-April or even May. March is still winter but boasts blue skies and brilliantly sunny days. Spring is condensed into two weeks of break-up: the mud season.

Fairbanks

Called the Golden Heart of the great Interior, Fairbanks is the hub for air, road, and river boat connections to many small villages scattered along Alaska's river systems. By our definition this is actually the heart of the real Alaska. It's home to all the romance and eccentricities of the north. Historian Bill Hunt, writing in the *Anchorage Daily News* says, "...Fairbanks is the Athens of Alaska, the state's undisputed intellectual and cultural center - and the envy of every wind-driven, money obsessed Anchoragite." Just an opinion, but we agree.

In March, the *North American Dog Sled Race*, the *Yukon Quest*, and the *Winter Carnival* are great places to meet real Alaska men. The weather at this time of year is absolutely perfect, just below freezing for perfect snow conditions, and always bright and sunny (for a full twelve hours starting with the equinox on March 21). In the *North American* twenty dog teams start right on Second Avenue downtown. There's lots of excitement. The whole event provides a great excuse for a party, and a great excuse for a winter trip. *Ice Alaska* invites ice carvers from all over the world and puts on a spectacular show of ice sculptures.

• *Howling Dog* in Fox (only open in summer) is the grandfather of all hangouts. On Friday nights it is purported to have the highest proportion of men to women of anywhere on the planet. Wear scruffy jeans to fit in, a red dress and spike heels to really get noticed. Prepare for serious rock and roll plus volleyball in the corral. And don't forget to take a nap, the action starts at midnight! Don't miss *Dawg House Pizza* in the back. Italian family style, absolute best pizza, in the state!

• *Thai House* is busy with the white collar crowd that holds serious meetings during lunch. It seems to be a favorite of the lawyers, good place to meet a single attorney. The tables are small and close, so lean over to the guy with the patagonia jacket over his suit coat and tie and ask for some help in locating your next destination.

• *Cafe de Par* boasts a sunny deck overlooking the Fairbanks Golf and Country Club... such as it is. Food's great. The golfing, no comment.

• *Pikes Landing* has a deck right on the river. A great summer hangout weekdays after 5 until the sun goes down around midnight. It's accessible by land, or by riverboat. In the winter, meet the snow machine, bush pilot, and air boat crowd in the lounge by the roaring fire in the stone fireplace.

his house

let's go inside

he's uptown - it's wired

breakfast

welding rod

boot grease

bullets

'never-seize' cutting oil

Your basic out-of-pocket-owner built home. The stairs aren't finished yet, but don't worry there's a rope to swing from. Hey, the phone works and there's a kitchen.

• *The Boatel* for darts, bridge, and off the wall conversation with strictly locals and college kids.

• *Pumphouse* on Chena Pump Road is the place to catch the university crowd, professors, doctors, and dentists in the homey, comfortable, but fake historic bar. In the summer, hoot and holler from the big deck at the passing river traffic.

• *The International Bar and Lounge* known locally as the Big "I", is for socializing on Friday or any other night. A great place to meet the labor union crowd. You might even sense an Irish lilt to the atmosphere.

• *Detours* or the *Greyhound Lounge* would be the place if you've got dancin' in your bones and want something other than sawdust under your feet, for the under 30 crowd.

• *Wood Center*, the student center at the University of Alaska Fairbanks is a time honored hangout spot. Students and others drop by to run into each other. Maybe you'll meet a handsome physics or environmental engineering professor.

• *Hot Licks* features the four basic food groups: ice cream, coffee, soup and bread. They make their own ice cream, plus espresso, and some-times feature jazz on Sunday nights. A friendly and casual gathering place for artists, writers, musicians, students, and the seasonally unem-ployed. It's laid back Fairbanks funk. Its sister hangout is the *Marlin*. Some coffee aficionados have defected to the *Alaska Coffee Company*.

• The *Whole Earth Food Store and Deli* is around the corner and down the block from Hot Licks. It features whole foods updated for the '90s and organic everything can be found here, including old hippies, new hippies, and those of us who have been diagnosed with new age ailments requiring new age remedies. Our favorite eligible public radio personality, Dr. Dave, is a frequent shopper and diner here. Good place to meet healthy, hip, 40plus Alaska men.

• *Bun on the Run* "Get your buns in here!" features great coffee, homemade pastries, and sandwiches served by two sisters from a circa 1950's trailer. Guests are seated outdoors on tree stumps (summer only). You can easily spend an entire afternoon here as everyone worth meeting in town stops by. One of the authors' favorite stops.

• *College Branch of the U.S Post Office* is a post office with atmosphere. While you're waiting to mail home your purchases, catch the locals just back from world traveling, or on their lunch break catching up on old news and new gossip.

• *Geophysical Institute* dominates the West Ridge of the UAF campus. Professors, scientists and grad students work here. You could inquire about future graduate work, research an article on volcanoes, or just snoop around!

• *Noel Wien Library* is home for seasonal workers brushing up on their winter reading . Try 10:30 or 11:00 am, right after *call* at the laborer's hall.

• *Fox Roadhouse* is a must for country swing dancing on Saturday nights. (Wear your cowgirl boots and ten gallon hat!) But for the really serious cowboy crowd, try the *Silver Spur*. You'll get met there.

• *The Turtle Club* in Fox is the place to catch some real Alaska atmosphere and monster hunks of Prime Rib. Big and tall men eat here.

• *Two Rivers Lodge* features gourmet dining, and a bar, the *Trappers Lounge,* that will give apoplexy to the save-the-animals crowd. Real Alaskans don't flinch.

•Canoe the lower Chena river right through downtown for a lazy afternoon float and a chance to attract the attention of all those riverboaters. End your trip at *Pikes* or the *Pumphouse.*

Further out of town from Fairbanks

• *Tacks Greenhouse* at 22 mile Chena Hot Springs Road is a nice place to stop for some home made pie or a great sandwich; it's also the center of a farming and dog mushing community. Mushers include the international set.

• Many locals like to canoe the upper Chena River, about 45 miles from Fairbanks on Chena Hot Springs Road in Chena River State Recreation area. It's mild white water, and some experience is a must. Great for fishing, too. Maps are available at *Tack's* on the way out, or stop at the Department of Natural Resources office in Fairbanks, and get directions from one of those cute Forestry guys.

• Hike the Angel Rocks Trail for a quiet view of the countryside and other local hikers.

• *Chena Hot Springs Resort,* about 60 miles from Fairbanks, is a nice excursion for a pleasant soak in the indoor pool, or the new outdoor Jacuzzi, especially in the winter.

• *Arctic Circle Hot Springs Resort* is about 135 miles from Fairbanks, over a mostly unpaved highway through the White Mountains.

Casually run into the local placer miners in the bar at the old time hotel, especially near the season's end (September - October).

• *Manley Hot Springs,* another popular excursion, is further afield on the Elliott Highway. During fall duck and moose season, it's the jumping off point to a rich hunting area. In fact, while driving there, you will be passed by pickup trucks full of men and their guns. You could get a flat tire, break a fan belt, who knows?

• *Manley Hot Springs Hotel,* the old one, is the place to meet local miners, outdoorsmen, and bush rats.

• Off the road system, Interior Alaska is the center for the rich diversity of the Athabaskan culture. Every year sees the introduction of new tours to Native villages like Huslia, Fort Yukon, and Arctic Village. To actually meet locals takes longer. If you have some camping and canoeing skills, you could plan a float trip down one of the rivers - Eagle to Circle on the Yukon, the bridge to Tanana on the Yukon, or Fairbanks to Manley on the Tanana River.

• For a real driving expedition, try the Haul Road (Dalton Highway) to *Coldfoot,* the furthest North truck stop. Stay overnight at the hotel, made up of converted Atco units, to get the flavor of the old pipeline camps. During hunting season you're likely to run into Alaska men who prefer hunting with bow and arrow. During every season you'll meet truck drivers, miners, sourdoughs, and permanent bachelors at this "manly" kind of place.

• *Chatanika Roadhouse* is a very Alaska place located on the Steese Highway, is a local hangout as well as one that attracts visitors. Great in winter. Those dashing Italian and French types who come to Fairbanks for winter adventure stop in here. The atmosphere

he's a true conservationist

Consider this an Alaska man's shopping mall.

His belt is fashioned from a conveyor belt from the Fairbanks sewage plant where he use to work.

He does his own sewing and repairs.

He can outfit himself for nothing. Just one more example of his conservationist philosophy.

DANGER
DO NOT ENTER
DUMPSTER

provides for easy eavesdropping and conversation. During the Christmas holidays, the interior is decorated top to bottom, moose antler to moose antler, with thousands of colored lights. For motorcycle enthusiasts, the owners' Harley Davidson is parked inside .

• To get the flavor of post pipeline, recycled Atco units, greasy spoon Alaska, stop at the Yukon River Bridge Crossing for lunch. If you're into health food, bring your own.

• In summer, the Yukon River Bridge Crossing on the Dalton Highway is the spot to catch a ride with *Yukon River Tours* and visit a traditional Indian fish camp while you tour this legendary river.

"You and Fairbanks have a lot in common, you're both cold, remote, and trashy."

Oregon woman visiting in June.

"Fox is a manly town. Everybody has a front end loader in their yard."

A Fox resident.

be prepared
to impress an Alaska man make sure you carry the essentials

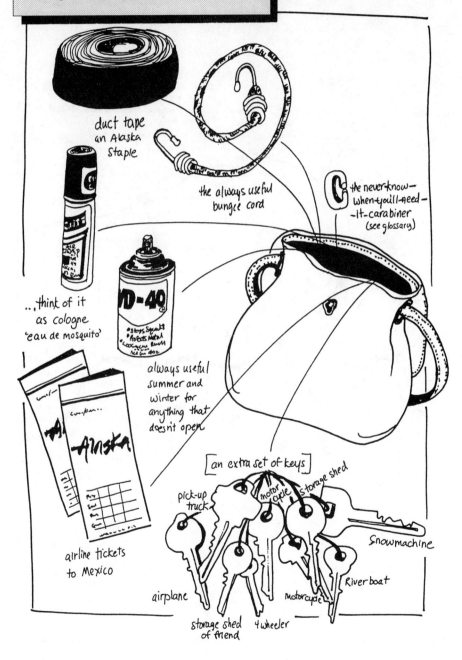

duct tape
an Alaska
staple

the always useful
bungee cord

the never-know—
when-you'll-need—
-it-carabiner
(see glossary)

...think of it
as cologne
'eau de mosquito'

always useful
summer and
winter for
anything that
doesn't open

airline tickets
to Mexico

[an extra set of keys]

pick-up
truck

motor
cycle

storage shed

Snowmachine

Riverboat

motorcycle

airplane

storage shed
of friend

4 wheeler

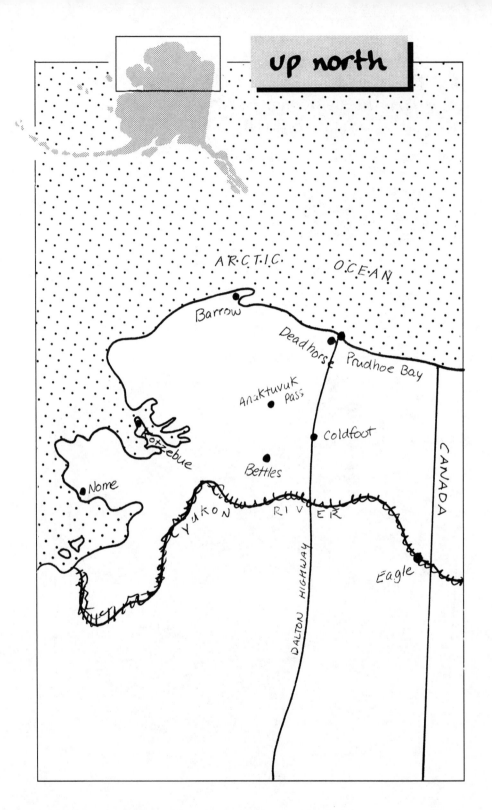

NORTHERN ALASKA

Northern Alaska includes the North Slope, the famous Brooks Range, and Northwestern Alaska, some of the most remote areas in the state. Sure it's hard to get to, but you can finally escape from the tourists.

Barrow

People who live in Barrow, where the sun never rises for three months in the winter, and never sets for three months in the summer, have spirit. Go for Spring Whaling, a real time of community sharing. Try the farthest north Mexican Restaurant.

Deadhorse

Deadhorse is the only place on the *slope* that is not strictly oil company controlled. It's the supply slum of the slope, and a truly manly place. You can fly in and stay in one of the hotels to get a real feel for the Alaska man's working experience. If you want to get hired as a bull cook, we hear it's best to apply before you leave Texas.

Nome

Nome is a gold rush ghost town, but there's little to be seen of the gold rush past. Today, it's known as the end of the Iditarod. For a great party, go for the end of the race in March. Lots of men in town: pilots galore, the who's who of mushers, veterinarians, celebrities, photographers, and reporters. The last are mostly women, scouting for an Alaskan man or the equivalent. We say be as aggressive as they are. Why not pretend you're a self-important New York correspondent too? March right up to the man you fancy and get a story. Make reservations early.

Everyone goes to *Fat Freddies* for breakfast, lunch and dinner. See and be seen. Don't forget to hang out at the race headquarters, another place of action. Night spots abound, try them all and find your favorite. Everyone talks about the *Board of Trade*. We don't exactly know what the appeal is, but if you pop in, you'll be able to talk about it too. The *Polaris Hotel* would be perfect for that sleazy flea bag hotel scene in your new novel, the one where your heroine encounters the drunk Russian sailor in the hallway with the peeling paint, musty, frayed carpet and bare light bulbs.

Kotzebue

East meets west, new meets old in Kotzebue, a jumping off point for the Noatak and Kobuk Rivers. Stroll up and down the beach in town, stand on the shore of the Bering Straits and gaze west to Siberia.

Bettles

From Fairbanks, charter a ride with a bush pilot to Bettles, one of the jumping off points for Brooks Range wilderness trips.

Eagle City

On the Yukon, almost in Canada, this is a tiny town where people go when they really want to get away from it all, live in a cabin, and trap. The all they're getting away from may include women!

Our Canadian Neighbors

Dawson City in the Yukon Territories, Canada, has been the great party town of the north since 1898. Dawson is the hub of the Klondike, and still home to rugged placer miners and gambling men at Diamond Tooth Gerties. To understand the flavor of the north and the psyche of the Alaska man, you need to visit Dawson City, see Jack London's cabin, listen to an actor re-create Robert Service's poetry in front of his old home, and *party*.

bachelor cabin up north

ice hook to
stop sled

dog harnesses
for the team

one window
design for
energy
efficiency –
he's saving
money on heat

sled to haul
supplies, like
water to and
from a nearby
creek

piles and
piles of
dog food

assorted
necessary
fluids - oil,
kerosene,
anti-freeze,
diesel

5 gallon buckets, as
popular as the 50
gallon drum - he can
never have too
many (used here for
food and water for
the dog team)

all building stops
in winter, but
he continues
to accumulate
materials

snow shoes for
breaking trail
for the dogs

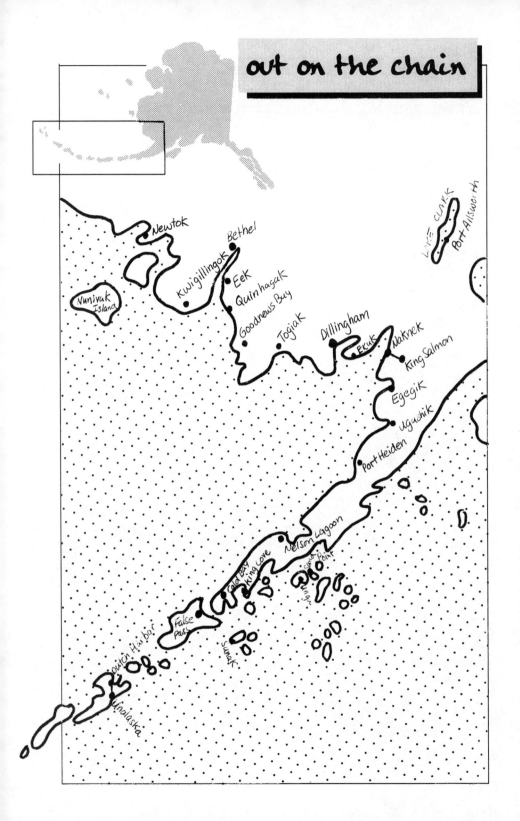

out on the chain

Newtok
Bethel
Kwigillingok
Eek
Quinhagak
Goodnews Bay
Togiak
Dillingham
Ekuk
Naknek
King Salmon
Egegik
Ugashik
Port Heiden
Nelson Lagoon
Sand Point
Cold Bay
King Cove
False Pass
Sanak
Akutan Harbor
Unalaska
Nunivak Island
LAKE CLARK
Port Allsworth

SOUTHWEST ALASKA

Southwest Alaska includes Bristol Bay and the Aleutian Chain, home of high stakes fishing, and the Yukon Kuskokwim delta, center of Yupik Eskimo culture. Thirty minute herring openings in this area can mean $200,000 in income in a half hour. The scenery here is high drama at its best, from striking weatherscapes against the lush rolling hillsides to the machismo of the inhabitants.

Unalaska/Dutch Harbor

This outpost on the Aleutian chain is the major port for the international high seas fisheries in the Bering Sea. Alaska's newest and most unlikely boomtown has an international flavor. No trees, but the magical hilly landscape varies with constantly changing weather and skies. The Bering Sea is the toughest and roughest fishing area in the world; consequently, it's a tough town, but it's hopping. It was once easy to get work, but now it's major industrial fishing with hiring done *outside*.

Dillingham

One of the southwest hubs for the largest commercial salmon fishing fleet in the world. It's also a jumping off place for area sports fishing lodges and rivers. The world-class sports fishing here attracts men.

• The *City Dock* is where the drift boats are docked, waiting for an *opening*. These are the high rollers. Suggested conversation topics for strolling the area: boat equipment or the weather, or time of the next opening, or what the season looks like compared to years past (usually never as good or better than ever). Or you could make some money selling homemade baked goods or even therapeutic massages; they all have bad backs and sore muscles. Also, seek out the location of the only free showers in town; men on one side, women on the other. It's a great place to strike up a casual conversation while waiting your turn.

• Bulletin boards at the local grocery stores are well read. You could advertise your foot and back massage services here.

• Everyone comes to the laundromat to wash clothes between openings. Thus, it's a hangout, with opportunity and plenty of time for a conversation. You could offer to help fold.

• Live music in the summer attracts fishermen, fisherwomen, crew, cannery workers, and fish processors. The best time to go is between openings. Everyone is on hold waiting to go fishing, so they are all are in a party mood, eager for fun and a good time. Be prepared to do nonstop dancing. You will be one of only a handful of women in a place packed with men. A yuppie-like atmosphere we think, but hey everything is relative in the bush!

• *Tent City* In early summer a lively crowd of mostly male students and hippies pitch their tents in Dillingham while waiting to get hired as crew members or cannery workers.

• The airport is one of the action spots in town. It's a tiny waiting room, mostly full of men coming to fish, going home from fishing, going hunting, or arriving for a job. It's the best place for an early introduction, as you'll see these faces in town throughout the season. The terminal itself will give you that first scent of the romantic, masculine fishy smell. Ahhh.

King Salmon

You leave from here to get to some of the world's best sports fishing. Men come here from all over the world to fish in the summer and hunt in the fall. It's also the gateway to Katmai National Monument *the* place to observe brown bears in their natural habitat. Katmai attracts professors and teachers who have the summers free and like nature photography.

• Again the airport waiting room is the place... sport fishermen abound here. The commercial fishing guys are here too as well as in the local coffee shop waiting for a herring opening or having just finished fishing, are counting their money. Before and after herring season is a good time to visit. If you're looking for work, be sure your conversation includes the following lines: "I enjoy rough seas." "I don't get sea sick." "I'm stronger than I look." "I'm not afraid to fly."

Bethel

This is the thriving center of the Yukon Kuskokwim Delta and center of Yupik' Eskimo culture. It's flat, treeless tundra, famous for 75 knot winds. There are young idealistic doctors at the YK Health Corporation who think they are on Northern Exposure, state and federal offices of attorneys, social workers, etc, and bush pilots.

• Meet everyone in town at the AC (Alaska Commercial Company store) or at the new Cultural Center. Or use the ubiquitous taxis to get around town. They try to carry as many passengers as possible on each trip so it's a great way to get an impromptu tour. There's great greek food at Dimitri's (we're not kidding!) And there's Diane's Cafe at the Pacifica Institute - a cross between a B&B and... something else.

• Events to catch are the Kusko 300 in January, a major dog sled race from Bethel to Aniak or the Camai Dance Festival in March, featuring Yupik' dance groups from all over the Delta.

Lake Clark / Port Allsworth

Home of folk hero, biologist, bush pilot, ex-governor turned actor, Jay Hammond, a member of the Alaska Man Hall of Fame. A beautiful location, and the home of the Inland Denaina Athabaskans. It's now another haven for sports fishing people and the entourages that go with them - guides, cooks, and the camp help.

more of the backyard

yes, the junk does have a purpose...

" the blue one matches the red one, and the white one matches the green one, which matches the one in the driveway..." He's explaining the logic of having a bunch of old vehicles in his yard. Matches means they provide parts for the other vehicle.

ACROSS THE STATE

More Good Ideas

• Lick a few envelopes at a campaign office in Juneau, Anchorage or Fairbanks. There's always some kind of campaign going on. If it's not an election year, find an initiative petition or recall drive! There's always one of these going on in Alaska; Alaskans love to get involved (read meddle with) their government. It's a great way to get to know Alaska's dedicated and not-so-dedicated politicos, and a variety of hangers-on. And they always go out afterwards for cappuccino or beer.

• Alaska has a very high per capita rate of home brew beer makers, mostly men. Check out the beer brewing supplies section of the local feed store in each of the larger communities in the state.

• Alaskans love their state fairs. Palmer and Fairbanks vie for the state fair title each year. The action in the southeast is at Haines. Each one is a terrific place to see our finest strolling around having a great time. Even more importantly, we guarantee you'll have a good time. We all have friends who come up every year from outside to experience this down home, true country celebration of community and midsummer.

• Every small town in Alaska has a wonderful old-fashioned Fourth of July celebration that tourists seem not to have discovered. Locals abound. Our favorites so far are in Seldovia, Eagle, Juneau, Douglas, Ester, Seward and McCarthy. You'll see the Alaska man hard at work in log rolling competitions, greased pole climbs, canoe jostling, etc. You may need to grab the nearest one for the three legged gunny sack race!

• If environmentalists or ardent pro-development types are your thing, you'll want to watch the local papers in each community for public hearing announcements. It's the best show in town, and there are always lots of people. It's a great way to find someone who shares your political persuasions. Stop and think about it. These are often great places to learn the most heartfelt values of the speaker *before* you make an emotional investment. And speaking of emotions, they usually run high on the kind of issues dealt with at hearings on the last frontier.

• If the athlete is your cup of tea, we would recommend stopping in at any sporting goods store in any community. Adopt a puzzled look near the pixies in the tackle section and see what happens next.

• The blue collar set can be found each weekday morning gathered at the union halls in all the major communities for union call. Casually stroll by and go in to use the bathroom.

• Don't forget the Post Office. It's the gathering place and information center, i.e. gossip swap, for every small town in the state. Some have bulletin boards inside or out; some have a paper back book trading corner; and all have a number of locals chatting about jobs, things for sale, travel, or their love life. Remember, the longer they've been in the community, the lower their post office box number. If you're looking for the seasoned type, linger at the section with box numbers 1 - 75.

Wanted

Single female Renter.
Good cook, mechanic,
Gardener, likes
hockey, cut firewood,
Split and stack it,
Canoe, Pack moose out.

Call Collect
Ask for Ron.

Another real-life want ad found by the authors
on a bulletin board in Fairbanks.
How thoughtful of Ron to accept collect calls.

Courtship
With
The
Alaska
Man

CHAPTER 4

what to do:
sports and activities

No matter what kind of Alaska man you find, once you start dating, sports and outdoor activities will become the focus. Every Alaska Man has his sport or sports, and he is totally devoted to them. It's part of their self definition. From ice-fishing to hockey, kayaking to ice-climbing, Alaska guys take their sports seriously. And, they want a woman to come along, come prepared and be ready to cope with the elements.

What follows are a few words on the specific Alaska bent found in each of the sporting activities you're likely to encounter. You may want to memorize this section. Most Alaska men are ever wary of the woman who cannot draw on the appropriate sports lingo when he suggests an outing. Trust us. When he first hints at a day trip to practice his favorite sport or two or three, he'll be watching closely for a confused or distasteful look from you, his potential victim. It's a test. If you pass it by nodding knowingly, or better yet, expounding briefly on, say, the benefits of white water kayaking over sea kayaking, you'll move beyond discussion to the next step in the courtship process - the excursion itself!

Boating

All kinds of boating are popular in Alaska. Every guy seems to have a boat: a simple aluminum canoe, a fancy sea kayak, a thirty foot river boat with a 150-horse jet engine, a rubber raft, a runabout or fishing boat, large or small. All the regular excursion and camping rules apply to boating trips. Make sure you have proper equipment, including adequate rain gear and a wool hat and gloves in all seasons. Make sure you have and wear a life jacket. True, you're going to look a little dopey by Lower 48 standards in one of those lumpy orange models, but better safe than sorry! If it really bothers you, get a fancy $40 dollar model that's more flattering.

River boating

This activity is very popular on all rivers in Alaska, and there are a lot of rivers. In the Interior, the Yukon is a wide superhighway, the Santa Monica Freeway of the bird flats. For fishing and hunting, or just for an excursion environmentalists paddle downstream in canoes, while the local aristocracy cruise in 30-foot aluminum riverboats with twin inboard jets. River boating is effortless for you, the passenger; just make sure you follow the survival rules at the end of this chapter and know where you are going. Wear sunglasses and take a good windbreaker with a hood, unless you like the windblown look.

Canoeing

More effort for you. Be sure you trust the guy you are going with - he will be steering. Don't go into white water with anyone who does not have previous experience. If in doubt about the difficulty, ask someone else, like a single forest ranger, or inquire at a public lands information office. The idea here is that you don't want to be downstream without a paddle when you decide you can't stand this guy. He can't just turn the boat around. So when he asks if you want to go on a canoe trip on the Porcupine River, be sure you can find the Porcupine River on the map. Oh yes, there it is, up there in the far right hand corner, 100 miles by air from Eagle. (Where's Eagle? Trust us, it's at least five major arguments away, if you're stuck with an inconsiderate lunatic.) Our advice: try a day trip first.

Kayaking: white water

See above rules for canoeing. The favorite white water kayaking spot in the Interior is the Nenana River Canyon, near Denali National Park. If you want to meet kayakers, head up there any weekend with your kayak. Kayakers will think you look most attractive in a dry suit and a helmet, after doing an Eskimo roll.

Sea-kayaking

This growing sport is a good way to see Kenai Fiord, Glacier Bay, or the Inland Passage. Excursions are available to the more popular spots. Be sure you know what you are getting into and that someone you are with has experience. Don't let yourself be talked into anything you think you can't handle. But if you get the chance, what could be more romantic (read *dangerous*) than seeing killer whales in Glacier Bay or Prince William Sound from a distance of ten feet.

River-rafting

One-day excursions are offered at a few of the most popular river rafting spots. Longer trips are offered by various guides and outfitters. This is a great way to see the wilderness, the real Alaska. Most of your companions will be other visitors to the state, but there are always the guides!

you're going on a weekend get-away

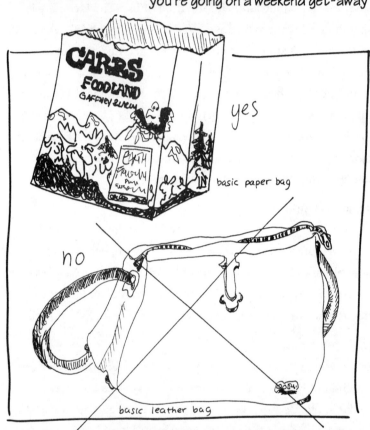

yes

basic paper bag

no

basic leather bag

you're going sailing

basic canvas slip-on

no

yes

basic PVC knee boot

Climbing

Climbers live in their own world. If you are one, or you want to be one, you can go straight to Talkeetna, the summer rendezvous for the Mt. McKinley climbers from all over the world.

Cycling

Mountain-biking is becoming more popular here every year. Check the cycling magazines for organized trips, or just show up with your bike. If you really want to acquire a fan club quickly, you could enter the *Iditabike*, the winter biking marathon that traverses 200 miles of the Iditarod Trail, acknowledged as the toughest mountain bike race in the world. "I needed something to do," said one female competitor of her decision to train by riding 100 miles a week all winter and then enter the race. This is but one example of what cabin fever will drive Alaska women to do. Of course, if this is you, welcome to heaven on earth.

Dog-mushing

Dog-mushing is the Alaska State Sport. Beyond the famous 1000 mile Iditarod Sled Dog Race (between Anchorage and Nome) in March, and the less famous but even tougher Yukon Quest (1000 miles between Fairbanks and Whitehorse), there are distance races (100-300 miles) all over the state, and many sprint races, including the Fur Rendezvous in Anchorage, and the North American in Fairbanks. All of these events provide a great excuse for a party, and a great excuse for a winter trip. Specifically, the Tudor Track in Anchorage and the Jeff Stoddard Race Grounds in Fairbanks are great places to catch the amateur action any winter weekend, with races for teams from one-dog to twelve. You can meet the dog-mushers there, or try one of the advertised excursions. If you're really serious, mushers are often looking for help at home with their kennels, which may have 50 to 100 dogs.

Fishing

What can we say about fishing? Whole books have been written on this subject. Everyone in Alaska loves fishing, to the tune of 317,000 fishing licenses in a state of 500,000 people. You can drop a line from any dock in the state. Fish in rivers accessible from the road system, fly in to a remote lake or fishing lodge, or charter for halibut or salmon. Go out in a riverboat on the Yukon, the Susitna, the Deshka, the Tanana, or countless other rivers. Dip-net for Kings and silvers in the Copper river at Chitna, or go ice-fishing on one of thousands of lakes in the winter.

Fish-camp

Fish-camp is a uniquely Alaska experience. The camp, consisting of multiple tents for sleeping and cooking, plus a smokehouse, is usually set up for a week or for the whole summer at a reliable fishing spot. The fish are caught in nets and smoked or canned on site as well. Fish camp is what might be called an "earthy experience" if you're into it, or just plain getting down and dirty, if you're not.

Fish-cutting

We guarantee you will gain his admiration and respect if you show up for that fishing trip with a really good filet knife that you know how to use. Don't be squeamish! Go right ahead and clean his fish and he'll think of you as someone it might be useful to have around. First grab the fish by the tail (if it's a reasonable size, (six or seven pounds), then whack its head on a rock to knock it out. Turning it on its back, slit the belly from the gills to the little hole at the rear end. Reaching into the belly cavity, rip its little guts out. In there are eggs (a large mass of translucent globules the size of small exquisite pearls). Save them, they're a delicacy. Clean the body cavity with water and your knife, then scrape off as many scales as you can. Now the fish is ready for your frying pan, and your male companion will likely be ready to propose marriage!

Gold-mining

Keep in mind that recreational gold-mining in Alaska is usually more for sport than a money-making venture. If your gorgeous hunk smells of diesel and has a wrench stuck in the pocket of his dirty overalls when he offers to take you out to his placer mine, be prepared for scenery that may look a little bit like a lunar landscape. Be emotionally prepared. He certainly won't appreciate it if, when you round that last bend and see his gold mine, you shout "Ugh! " and chastise him for despoiling the wilderness. Try to keep in mind the historical perspective. Most areas currently mined by placer miners have actually been mined once or even twice before. Some of the areas being mined today have been worked since the 1880s. Also remember that most placer mining today involves spending 10 percent of the time running around in heavy equipment and 90 percent fixing the equipment when it breaks down. Bring your cards and that old copy of *War and Peace* you've been meaning to reread.

cutting fish

Hiking

Every community in Alaska offers various day-hikes close to town. In Juneau, lovely trails are available by just walking out of town. Mountain hikes can be taken within the Anchorage city limits. In Fairbanks, good hiking trails are 20 or 30 miles out. See the U.S. Forest Service office, or the nearest Alaska Public Lands Information Center for detailed information about hiking and camping. Keep in mind that a good pair of sturdy hiking boots and good rain-gear are always advisable, as well as a warm jacket or sweater. Anywhere in Alaska, a sudden storm can bring cool temperatures even on a sunny day. Who will you meet? Other hikers!

Hunting

If asked, more than 80 percent Alaska men would consider themselves hunters. (More than 102,000 hunting licenses were issued in 1987, out of a total population of 500,000). Most of these hunters are men. Will they want to take you hunting? Probably not. (See Duck Widow in the glossary). Hunting is usually done as an elaborate ritual of male bonding. If invited, you may want to choose not to go on one of these ritual moose hunts. But some women do. In fact, a few Alaska women have become legendary hunters. One early Alaska pioneer, Fanny Quigley, found herself stranded on a cold winter evening after felling a moose with no shelter from the deathly cold, she had no alternative but to open the carcass and crawl in for warmth until the storm blew over.

Ice-climbing

If you have any experience rock-climbing and you're around in the winter, you'll want to try out this variation, which involves climbing frozen waterfalls. Valdez, with its spectacular Thompson Pass, is a center for this activity. If seeing athletic young men in those wild lycra tights appeals to you, then you might want to travel to Valdez for the ice-climbing festival and competition in February. There you'll meet climbers from all over the world.

Running

This is a popular sport statewide in summer and it's growing in winter, too. Short 5- and 10-K races are held all summer. Running clubs that engage in two- or three-day relay road races in summer are a great way to meet people. Check the bulletin boards at sports stores. All of these races provide fabulous mix and meet opportunities worth training for. We highly recommend the Fairbanks Midnight Sun Run. Held every year at midnight as close to summer solstice (June 21) as the calendar will allow, this is a truly zany costume event that attracts thousands with its late-night party atmosphere.

Skiing, downhill

Tommy Moe. What more can we say? The skiing at Alyeska Ski Resort continues through May. Alyeska, the largest ski resort in the state, is located 20 miles south of Anchorage in the community of Girdwood. At Eaglecrest near Juneau you'll meet legislative staffers on the slopes letting their hair down for a few weekend hours before they head back to the hallowed halls of the capitol. And to meet the truly adventurous downhiller, go to Valdez and experience extreme skiing. Take a helicopter to the top of some of the tallest slopes in Thompson Pass and ski down some of the steepest slopes you'll ever encounter. Again, unless you're in the world-class category, it may be better to be a spectator on this one. In Fairbanks, catch the extreme ski types and the telemarkers on the ungroomed steep downhills at Ski Land. Or if you want to keep the *do* in place, head for the well laid out, groomed slopes at Fairbanks' newest ski area, Moose Mountain, where you can avoid freezing by using their unique terrestrial trams.

he's arts and craftsy

hand work

a sculptural walkman using found materials

He can express himself in thread, rope, and steel.

YUKON RIVER

State of Alaska cut out of steel from the transalaska oil pipeline

Skiing, cross-country

This is especially hot in Fairbanks and Anchorage. Fairbanks features perfect conditions and dry snow from October til May, with many miles of touring trails, and 25-K of good groomed trails at Birch Hill, where skating is the rage. Anchorage has many miles of world-class groomed trails within city limits at Kincaid and Russian Jack parks, as well as ski mountaineering and touring in the Chugach National Forest, which is virtually in town. The height of the ski season is in March, when temperatures are milder and the sun a constant companion.

Ski-mountaineering

Spring is the season for well-planned trips in the Chugach Mountains near Anchorage, and in the Alaska Range between Anchorage and Fairbanks. A variety of outfitters lead guided expeditions. Try ski-mountaineering clubs associated with the University of Alaska Fairbanks, Anchorage, or Southeast in Juneau for a healthy exposure to the student set. The average age of University of Alaska students is thirty.

Snow-machining

This is a very popular winter sport. Dress warmly. A one piece insulated snow machine suit in dark green is de-rigueur and will hide any irregularities in your figure. These people don't know when to quit. Some of them keep going even at 35 below zero. The Arctic Man Competition at Summit Lake in the Alaska Range marks the height of the spring season. Here Alaska men turn out en masse to ride through the untracked, treeless tundra. They party and watch the main event, where a skier gets towed behind a snow machine at 70 mph.

Wind surfing

Anyone's year of living dangerously could include wind surfing in Turnagain Arm, where it joins Cook Inlet. World-record tides, 33 degree water, and sudden weather changes seem to enhance the excitement. Recommended for this location: just watch. It's truly dangerous. Wind surfing is also popular on lakes all over the state throughout the summer. Remember to bring your wet suit. Or try a tamer, but chillier version of this exotica by wind skating on Wasilla Lake midwinter.

Winter camping

Very popular among the dog-mushing and mountaineering set. Proper equipment is essential, as is common sense. Every year a few people lose a few toes in silly accidents, caused by leaving on a skiing trip too late in the day or when the weather looks chancy. If you do decide to go, and you heed all of our advice, you'll find yourself in a winter wonderland, as sunny and full of wide-open spaces as any deserted island paradise.

"He brought a deck of sandwiches. It turned out to be a loaf of bread with a slab of moose meat between each slice."

Gourmet picnic with an Alaska man.

"Alaska men are the kind of men that inspire country western songs like 'I'm Just a Road Kill on the Highway of Your Love.'"

Waitress at the Silver Spur.

CAUTION

On a more serious note, please don't simply rely on one of the "trust me" guys. If your intuition tells you not to go on a somewhat chancy expedition, don't go. You might miss a good trip, or you might miss a disaster.

Rest assured that wherever you go in Alaska, a nearby quaint little inn for lunch or dinner is unlikely. Almost anywhere anyone wants to go to do anything requires camping out. Car camping, RV camping, canoe camping, backpacking, hunting, fishing, riverboat camping, airplane camping; whatever you are going to be doing, you are going to be out in the wilderness. A few general rules apply to all activities, all of the time:

1. Know where you are going. Look at the map, familiarize yourself with the area.

2. Make sure someone at home or home base knows where to look for you and when you will be back. Write it down for them.

3. Make sure you have proper equipment, layers of clothing including adequate rain gear and warm clothing. Including wool hat and gloves, in any season.

4. If you are camping, or if there is a possibility you might get stuck overnight, make sure you have a warm sleeping bag, sturdy tent, extra clothing, matches, and food.

5. If you are going anywhere in the winter, even in a car, make sure there is a sleeping bag, and an extra pair of warm coveralls and winter boots in the car.

Don't trust someone you just met to make adequate preparations. Check everything yourself. Don't worry about looking stupid. If he's the right kind of guy, he'll respect you for this.

So remember, find out where you'll be going, how far, and for how long. What's his experience, has he been there before. Make sure you have adequate equipment, food, matches, sleeping bags, and warm clothing. Make sure you have a map, and that someone in town knows exactly where you are going and when you will be back.

CHAPTER 5

sex and the Alaska man

We can't have a book about Alaska men without a chapter on sex... can we?

Since this is the 90's we decided to convene a focus group. We asked them, "What is special, unique, distinct, and different about sex and the Alaska man?" To our amazement our focus group members, women from all walks of Alaska life, agreed on one thing: Alaska men like sex!

And what makes sex with an Alaska man so special? Location, location, location.

four rules for making love in a tent:

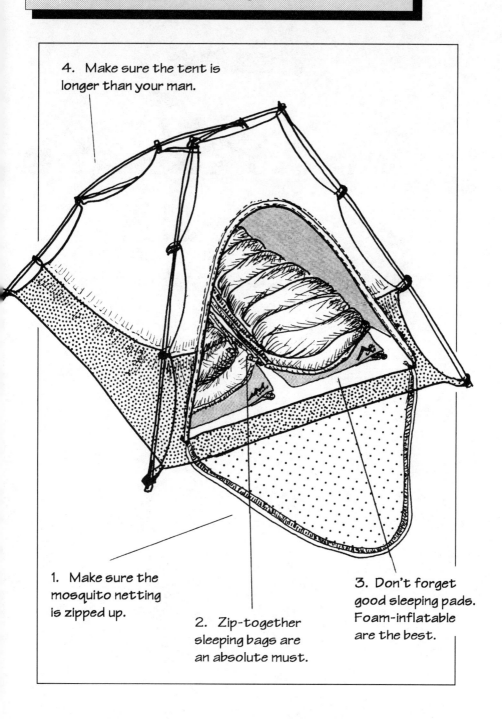

4. Make sure the tent is longer than your man.

1. Make sure the mosquito netting is zipped up.

2. Zip-together sleeping bags are an absolute must.

3. Don't forget good sleeping pads. Foam-inflatable are the best.

Appendix: Survival Tools

am I really looking for an Alaska man?

Am I really ready for the great northern adventure? Can I handle true love in the land of the midnight sun? Am I ready for multiple encounters with this northern species known as the Alaska man? To find out, take a shot at answering these questions.

think about it...

get some insights quiz

1. After a hunting trip, an Alaska man is likely to:

    a. have experienced duck bonding

    b. have enough material for years of tall-tale telling with the other guys

    c. have lots of excuses as to why he didn't actually shoot anything

    d. come home with an injury

2. If your Alaska man works on the North Slope:

    a. he makes a lot of money

    b. you don't have to spend much time with him

    c. he doesn't have a future

    d. all of the above

3. Alaska has the third highest divorce rate because:

    a. women leave their husbands and return to the lower 48

    b. women leave their husbands to go back to school

    c. women leave and go home to their mothers

    d. men leave their women to spend more time with their dogs

4. If he was as successful outside as he says he was, what is he doing in Alaska?

    a. running away

    b. looking for something

    c. finding something

    d. running from the law

    e. avoiding the stress of success

5. What is the best method for getting a car unstuck?

a. use a shovel

b. use chains

c. rock it out

d. use kitty litter

e. use ashes

6. What will your mother think when she hears he lives alone in an 8x10 cabin with 7 dogs, no running water, a dirt floor, and is 100 air miles from the nearest neighbor?

a. he's crazy

b. he loves dogs

c. he's finding himself

d. thank God she's finally found a man

7. What skills are needed to meet/catch an Alaska man?

a. ability to speak his language

b. good listening skills

c. ability to dress game and clean fish

d. a good job

8. What qualifications are necessary to keep an Alaska man?

a. having a job

b. having a job

c. having a job

d. getting an inheritance

e. don't mention his getting a job

"After the first winter I got her her own cabin with a port a potty."

Alaska man on thoughtfulness.

9. How much did that Moose steak you had for dinner really cost?

a. don't ask

b. three weeks of lost salary

c. one smashed front end on the $20,000 four-wheel-drive pickup you bought for him

d. $600 to charter the Super Cub to fly him out

e. one year's interest payments on the $30,000 loan for the plane

10. What do you need to get rid of an Alaska man?

a. a social disease

b. another Alaska man

c. children

d. stop working

e. mention the "C" word

11. What else could you do to get rid of an Alaska man?

a. introduce him to one of your friends

b. suggest he get a real job

c. tell him you don't like his pick-up

d. send him to town for a case of beer

12. How much does a cord of firewood cost?

a. $350 for a good chainsaw

b. $150 for new Carharts

c. $20,000 for a new pickup after destroying the transmission on the old one

d. All of the above

"Rotate to avoid infestation."

Alaska man's theory on food storage.

13. Those stripes on the back of his jacket are:

a. a fashion statement

b. battery acid stains from carrying his car battery into the cabin each night for warming by the wood stove

c. reflector tape

d. duct tape to repair the damage from the latest handyman project

14. How many Alaska men does it take to change a light-bulb?

a. no more than one; any more than that and they'll argue about it until spring, and by then you won't need the light anyway.

b. none if you don't have electricity

c. what light bulb?

15. When an Alaska man dresses up, he:

a. looks like someone you wouldn't want to be seen with

b. puts on his clean Carharts

c. scrapes the fish slime off his hip waders

d. scrapes the dog excrement off his Sorrels

16. Stalking the Alaska man is like:

a. stalking a wiley trout

b. bear baiting

c. snagging a salmon with a treble hook

d. all of the above

"With a little duct tape and plastic I can create or repair just about anything."

The always frugal, inventive, and practical Alaska man.

think about it quiz

Answer Yes or No

1. Do you want to spend the rest of your life supporting a bush pilot, student or artist?

2. Can you skin a moose, butcher it, and pack it out before it gets dark?

3. Are you prepared to live in an out-of-pocket house on old mine tailings?

4. Is talking about, preparing for, going on, and reminiscing about a hunting or fishing trip your idea of a good time?

5. Can you hold your own in a conversation about outdoor equipment?

6. Do you think men look really sexy in insulated overalls, down jackets, hats, gloves and heavy boots?

7. Can you drive the following:

    a. fork lift

    b. 4 X 4

    c. 6 X 6

    d. skiff

    e. tour bus

    f. plane on skis

    g. dog sled

    h. back hoe

    i. RV

    j. 18 wheeler

    k. plane on skis

    l. snow machine

    m. pickup truck

    n. jet ski

    o. air boat

    p. plane on wheels

    q. van

    r. 4 wheeler

    s. 4 wheeler pulling a trailer

    s. plane on floats

    t. dog truck

> "In a couple of hundred years his yard will be mined for the minerals."
>
> In time he could be worth something.

Know your numbers quiz

1. **206**

    a. being late for lunch

    b. a six seater airplane

    c. safety device for boats

    d. a medium size halibut

    e. a good size salmon

    f. an overweight plane

2. **6 sack with a 4 inch slump :**

    a. a set of luggage after it's been to the North Slope

    b. a northern term for a beer belly

    c. the amount of cement per yard of concrete and the percent of moisture added.

    d. number of salmon allowed per sport fishing charter

3. **325**

    a. number of miles from Fairbanks to Anchorage

    b. his SAT score

    c. the average price of gold per ounce

    d. the average Alaska male's weight

    e. your weight after one winter in the north

    f. the flight number that takes him back to his mother

"I came up here to get away from women. I'm not looking for one."

He's being direct.

4. 800

   a. your favorite phone numbers

   b. the length of the Transalaska Oil Pipeline

   c. the cost of a plane ticket back home

   d. the length of a halibut skate

   e. the number of fathoms the anchor on your set net line will fall

   f. the engine size of his snow machine

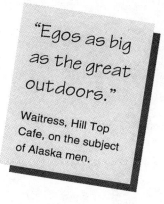

"Egos as big as the great outdoors."

Waitress, Hill Top Cafe, on the subject of Alaska men.

5. 6 - 8 - 10

   a. types of aircraft

   b. combination to his gym locker

   c. numbers used with the letter D to denote models of caterpillars

   d. all of the above

6. 13

   a. the average foot size of an Alaska man

   b. day of the month to pickup the unemployment check

   c. average number of kids per family in Hydaburg

   d. an IFQ quota

   e. a signal to leave the party

   f. the number of semesters he has left to complete his degree

His seat covering means:

a. he cares about appearances

b. it covers the hole in the seat

c. he keeps important papers filed here

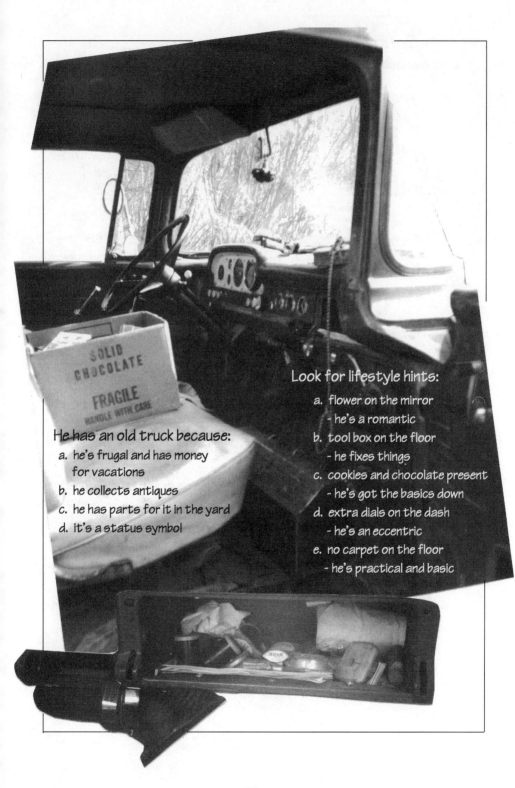

SOLID
CHOCOLATE

FRAGILE
HANDLE WITH CARE

He has an old truck because:

a. he's frugal and has money
   for vacations
b. he collects antiques
c. he has parts for it in the yard
d. it's a status symbol

Look for lifestyle hints:

a. flower on the mirror
   - he's a romantic
b. tool box on the floor
   - he fixes things
c. cookies and chocolate present
   - he's got the basics down
d. extra dials on the dash
   - he's an eccentric
e. no carpet on the floor
   - he's practical and basic

He drives a DORF truck because:

a. it's a way to express his creativity

b. to attract other Alaska men

c. he's embarrassed to drive a Ford

d. it's been passed down to him by another Alaska man

e. it runs

What does he carry in his attaché cases?

a. zip lock bags of papers, files, and information

b. his necessary day equipment like camera, film, and welding goggles for driving directly into the sun

c. lunch

Note: These are not just 5 gallon buckets. These are 5 gallon buckets turned attaché cases. They pack and carry well.

quiz scoring

Part One: Multiple choice:

1/a, b, c, d 2/d 3/a, b, c, d 4/e 5/c 6/a 7/a 8/a 9/a
10/d 11/a, b, c, d 12/d 13/d 14/b 15/b 16/d

Part Two: Yes or No Questions

For each YES answer, pack another item in your suitcase

For each NO answer, unpack something from your suitcase

Part Three: Know Your Numbers

1/b 2/c 3/a 4/b 5/c 6/a

the results

If you were right most of the time:
   You don't even need this experience,
   move to New Mexico or Hawaii.

If you thought we were mostly kidding:
   You might enjoy it.

If you missed most of the questions:
   You have no idea what you're getting into.

glossary:
need-to-know Alaska terms

We have this glossary in our little guidebook because we have all noticed that many women who visit Alaska spend a lot of their time trying to interpret what Alaska men are saying, rather than being able to work on other more important communication goals!

A-List
The top list at the Union hall. A high number on the A-list means an early chance to be called out to work on what is usually a well-paid job.

AFN
Alaska Federation of Natives.

Alaska Time
Late.

ANCSA
Alaska Native Claims Settlement Act, the landmark indigenous people's land claims legislation passed in 1971 to facilitate construction of the pipeline.

ANWR
(Pronounced An-war). The Alaska National Wildlife Refuge on the north slope.

ARCO
Atlantic Richfield Co., also known as Big Oil.

ATCO Units
Portable housing, i.e. trailers, used as work camps during the pipeline. Now recycled as 'lodges' around the state.

Baling wire
Seen everywhere and useful for fixing anything at all. Also a descriptive term for anything jerry-rigged together, as in, "put together with baling wire."

Beards
Ubiquitous on Alaska men.

Belly dump
A type of dump truck pulled by a semi-truck which dumps from hinged doors under the belly of the trailer, and usually driven by a well-paid teamster.

BP
British Petroleum Co., the other half of Big Oil.

Break-up
When the ice on the rivers cracks into huge chunks, signaling the coming of spring and the opening of boating season. Also, mud season, that time in spring when the snow melts.

Break-up boots
High top rubber boots for navigating puddles and mud during break-up; known as milking boots in the Midwest.

Boomer
One who believes that the next big money development project is coming any day.

Brooks Range
A range of mountains running East to West dividing the North Slope from the rest of Alaska. Named after Alfred E. Brooks, an early geologist.

Bunny boots
Use-to-be Army issue big white round rubber winter footwear, also known as VB Boots for Vapor Barrier. Don't even try to worry about appearing attractive in these puppies!

Bush
That part of Alaska that is remote and accessible only by air, dog-team, or boat.

Bush rat
One who lives in the bush and only comes out occasionally, looking just like a drowned...

Bush teacher
A teacher at a school in a remote village.

Cabin fever
A mental health disorder (related to claustrophobia) acquired after living too long in a small cabin in the middle of the winter in the middle of nowhere with nowhere to go.

Carabiner
A clip used in mountain climbing and dog-mushing.

Cat
A bulldozer.

Chains
The kind you need for your car or truck tires on snow and ice.

Cheechako
One new to Alaska or the far north.

Chinook
A King Salmon, the grand daddy of them all in terms of size, not taste.

Chum
A Dog Salmon.

Coho
A Silver Salmon.

Cleanup
The entire effort to cleanup the Valdez oil spill. Or, in gold-mining terminology, to take apart one's sluice box and recover the gold.

Commitment
Not present in the Alaska Man's vocabulary.

Components
Parts that will come in handy someday. Will look like junk and trash to you.

Conservationist
The Alaska man that's here to stay. He has a yard, a shed, and a house full of recyclables.

Cord
A cord of wood is 4' x 4' x 8'. If he's cutting green birch and you're hauling and stacking, its going to seem three times as big. You have no idea how *much* wood this is!

Crude
Crude oil. As in, "Let's go to Naked Island and get crude," meaning let's get hired onto the cleanup effort on Naked Island (an Island in Prince William Sound) to clean up crude oil.

D-10
One of the larger Caterpillar bulldozers.

D-8
A slightly smaller version.

> "Those aren't spare parts in his yard, it's a religious shrine to his grandmother's memory. He's still deifying her."
>
> A woman in the know.

128

DADS

A group of fathers in the Mat-Su area who feel they have been wronged in custody and child-support matters, and it's going to be expensive.

Denali

The Indian name for Mt. McKinley meaning the High One.

Dividend Check

The Alaska Welfare check that is paid to all who manage to just stay here. Pass GO collect close to $1,000 each year. Alaska's Permanent Fund pays a dividend every year to all Alaskans.

Dog Lot

Home of the 50 or so dogs a good musher keeps in his kennel, all chained to their dog houses, as in "Smells like a dog lot."

Double wall

A house built with two exterior walls, about 8" thick, and a foot apart for extra insulation.

Duck widow

An Alaska woman left at home while her guy is out duck hunting.

Duct tape

A thick gray tape that is believed by all Alaska men, and most Alaska women, to fix almost anything, including kayaks, duffel bags, sleeping bags, his bunny boots, your ballet shoes, and even the heating ducts for which it is named.

Equinox

March 21 and September 21, the two days every year when the sun crosses the equator and Alaska has 12 hours of daylight and 12 hours of night.

Exxon Valdez

The name of the super tanker whose grounding on Bligh Reef caused the Prince William Sound Oil Spill.

Fish wheel

An ingenious contraption similar to a perpetual motion machine for catching salmon using the river current.

Fixer-upper

A house or cabin that "needs a little work."

Five-eights

A forty-hour work week, five eight-hour days (an unusually light schedule for the summer months in a dramatically seasonal economy).

Four-by-four

A truck or car with four wheel drive, or a piece of lumber four inches by four inches in cross section.

Four wheeler

A motor scooter with four wheels

Freeze-up

When winter arrives and all of Alaska freezes; mud, rivers, plumbing - everything.

Frost heave

Occurs when frozen saturated soil expands; can crack concrete slabs and basements, or heave pilings and telephone poles out of the ground.

Fur Rendezvous

Big winter festival in Anchorage, also known as Rondy.

Gates, The

Short for Gates of the Arctic National Park in the Brooks Range.

Gee

Dog-mushing command meaning "Kindly turn right, Fido": opposite of Haw.

Gill-net

A fish net that catches fish by trapping them around the gills.

Gold pan

A large diameter flat metal pan like a pie pan, used for panning gold by washing stream gravels and shaking the pan in a circular motion.

Gold pan painting

A popular folk art form: Alaska scenes such as a cabin in winter are painted on a gold pan that is eventually hung on a wall.

Grateful Dead

They're coming to Fairbanks this summer for sure. Right. Actually, a Fairbanks sculptor has been commissioned by the rest of The Dead to do Jerry's head in bronze.

Grizzly

A large brown bear with ferocious reputation; also, mechanical shaker for separating large and small rocks in placer mining.

Handyman Special

See fixer-upper.

Harness

As in dog-harness.

Haul Road, The

The original road to Prudhoe Bay, now the Dalton Highway.

Haw

A dog-mushing command meaning "Let's turn left here": opposite of Gee

Hazelwood, Joe

Ill-fated captain of the ill-fated oil tanker, the *Exxon Valdez*.

Headbolt heater

A device for heating up your engine block in cold weather.

Homesteading

Acquiring title to land the hard way, by building a habitable dwelling and living there.

Honey bucket
Type of toilet which must be emptied out back.

Hot springs
Where hot water comes seeping out of the ground.

Humpie
A Pink Salmon.

Hundred-mile-an-hour-tape
Duct tape. It keeps his airplane together while going 100mph.

Ice fog
Winter condition when car emissions settle close to the ground in below zero temperatures. The water vapor freezes causing a dense, eerie fog.

Iditarod
A gold-rush ghost town, a trail, and a famous dog sled race.

Jay
Jay Hammond, ex-governor.

Jerry-rig
To fix something by making do with what you have on hand, a common practice in remote parts of the state.

Job
A money making opportunity for the convenience of the Alaska man who needs to earn a grubstake between fishing and hunting seasons.

Jumping a trap line
To trap in someone else's territory.

Jumping a claim
To claim gold mining ground previously staked by someone else.

King
King Salmon, see Chinook.

Klondike
The river by this name is a tributary of the Yukon. The region, in Northern Yukon Territories, Canada, was the scene of the Klondike Gold Rush of 1898. A term that has come to mean great wealth of any kind (see also Bonanza, Eldorado).

Libby
Libby Riddles, the first woman to win the Iditarod Sled dog Race.

Libertarian
A political party founded on the right to do whatever you want, whenever you want.

Loader
A piece of heavy equipment, front-end loader.

Longevity bonus
Monthly income given to all Alaska seniors just for staying here.

Lottery land
Occasionally the state sells off choice parcels of land by lotteries.

Lower 48
The continental United States.

Mary
Mary Shields, the first woman to finish the Iditarod Sled Dog Race.

Midnight sun
You really can see it at midnight north of the Arctic Circle.

Minute
Alaskan definition of eternity. As in, "I'll have this (car, furnace, snow-machine, boat motor, etc.) fixed in a minute."

Moose nuggets
You know, moose droppings. Sometimes painted gold and made into jewelry. Can you believe it?!

Mukluks
Native Alaska footwear made of sealskin, caribou, or moosehide.

Mush
To travel by dog team. Also, command for dog-team to moveit.

Nordstroms
Alaskan for shopping: As in "I'm going to Anchorage to do Nordstroms."

North, Up
On the North Slope, or North of the Brooks Range, as in "He's up north."

"You know the type, the old eccentric guy that lives at the edge of town... well my Alaska man is apprenticing to become that social outcast."

Kenai woman on her man's aspirations.

North Slope
Technically, the northern slope of the Brooks Range. Colloquially, the whole area north of the Brooks Range to the Arctic Ocean, including Barrow, the oil fields at Prudhoe Bay, and ANWR.

Nuggets, moose
See Moose nuggets.

Nuggets, gold
Large chunks of gold.

Okies
The Oklahoma-type pipeliner who shows up in Fairbanks in the winter with a ten gallon hat and cowboy boots that have been sprayed with urethane foam for insulation.

Opening
The time determined by the state when it is legal to commercial fish a specific species within a specific area. Generally a 6- to 72-hour period. In other words you've got to work fast.

Operator
Heavy equipment operator, member of the Operators Union.

ORV
Off road vehicle.

Out house
Outside facilities, toilet.

Outside
America, the Lower 48, the rest of the U.S.

Panning
Using a gold pan to "test the colors" of a stream; in other words, trying to find gold.

Parka
A warm winter jacket long enough to come down to your knees, usually sports a hood with fur trim.

Permafrost
Permanently frozen ground that is dangerous to build on due to seasonal instability.

Permanent Fund
Alaska's collective $17 billion plus oil revenue savings account.

Pink
A variety of salmon.

Pioneer
Longtime Alaska resident.

Pioneer's Home
An old age home for pioneers.

Pipeline, the
The transalaska oil pipeline running from Prudhoe Bay to Valdez .

Pipeline widow
The little lady left in town while her old man is up on the slope doing his

seven-twelves, nine on and two off,
at Prime Camp.

Pipeliner
Someone who came to Alaska in the
mid-70s to build the TransAlaska
pipeline; usually a union hand.

Placer mining
Mining for gold which has collected
in the gravel stream beds of interior
Alaska and the Yukon Territories.

Plug-in
Here in the far north, it gets so cold
in winter you need special engine
heaters for your car. Thus you have
to "plug your car in" for a few hours
before starting it. True luxury is
having, both at home and at work, a
socket to plug into.

Pom-pom
Looks like the real cheerleader thing,
but made of absorbent material and
used to clean up the Valdez oil spill.
May still be seen on beaches in Prince
William Sound.

Quonset hut
A barrel shaped prefab military
structure, many of which are still
around. Not generally habitable,
no matter what he tries to tell you.

R and R
Rest and relaxation, i.e., time off
from the pipeline to go to Bali or
somewhere warm.

Real House
The kind with plumbing, bedroom
doors, and a dishwasher.

Red Dog
The world's largest lead-zinc mine,
located north of Kotzebue. Also a
Juneau Saloon.

Refrigerwear
Insulated coveralls

Rocking out the car
Alternately putting the car into
first gear and reverse, while
everyone else pushes to get it out
of a ditch or snow bank.

Ruff
Fur trim around a parka hood to
assist in breathing in exceptionally
cold temperatures.

RV
Recreational Vehicle, i.e., elaborate
camper.

SAD
Seasonal Affective Disorder, a
seasonal depression caused by lack
of light.

Sauna
Finnish bathing custom, consisting of
a small room or building in which
rocks are heated by a wood stove.
Bathers get sweaty and then jump in
the snow or a cold lake to cool off.

Seasonal
A job which lasts only through one season.

Seasons
May, June, July, August and winter.

Seiner
A type of fishing boat.

Set-net
A type of fish net which is set in a particular spot.

798-ers
They live and work all over the world on short pipeline jobs. They mostly speak with a drawl and a good number have forty acres and a mule somewhere in Missouri. No women or minorities, except a few Oklahoma Indians, all of whom are known as *Chief*.

Seven-twelves
Working hours consisting of twelve hours a day, seven days a week .

Sex
Mating ritual refined only by isolated and remote segments of the human population in the far north.

Shoe-pacs
A form of winter foot-gear consisting of an outer leather boot with a rubber shoe and sole, and an inner boot made of wool felt.

Short call
A union call for a job of two weeks or less, which you can take without losing your number on the A-list.

Sierra clubber
Considered by most long-time Alaskans to be a panty-waist who "cares more about the environment than the rugged individualists who choose to live here." Usually someone from outside. (See tree-hugger).

Skating
Cross country skiing technique.

Slope, the
See North Slope.

Snagging
Illegal technique for catching salmon.

Snow-go
A snow machine.

Snowbird
A seasonal Alaska worker who defects to Hawaii for the winter and returns in spring with the rest of the migrating waterfowl, as in "Here today, gone to Maui."

Sockeye
A Red Salmon.

Solstice
June 21 and December 21, the longest and shortest days of the year,

135

respectively. Important Alaskan holidays.

Sorels
A trade name for shoe pacs.

Sourdough
A long-time Alaskan. Don't ask.

Southeast Sneaker
Goodyear knee-high rubber boots.

Spawn-till-you-die
Famous Alaska motto.

Spenard Divorce
Finalized when one of the spouses gets shot.

Steve
Steve Cowper, ex-governor; aka the high-plains-drifter.

Subsistence
A complex concept, in terms of regulatory definition, of living off the land.

Sun-dog
Meteorological occurrence of vertical rainbows on either side of the sun near the horizon.

Superinsulated
Home built with extra insulation, like walls twelve inches thick, in order to use less heat.

Susan Butcher
Woman who has won the most long distance sled dog races in Alaska.

Tailings
Gravel piles that are the remains of mining operations.

Termination dust
The first snow of each winter; refers to the cheechako's tendency to leave the state when the first snow flies.

The Big One
Denali, Mt. McKinley.

Three wheeler
Three-wheel off-road motor scooter.

Tony
Tony Knowles, governor.

Trapline chatter
A radio program that broadcasts personal messages to bush folks who have no telephones.

Trolling
Fishing from a slowly cruising boat / see also, cruising the bars / see also, looking for a date.

Up North
On the North Slope.

Vacation
You're going to need one of these every winter.

VECO
An oil field service company and large employer. Politically incorrect.

Visqueen
Polyethylene plastic sheeting, used for everything from home building to covering the compost pile and the garden beds to greenhouses and temporary shelters. You may need to use it with duct tape to fashion emergency weatherproof clothing or create unique art-to-wear pieces for the local arts group event.

Wally
Wally Hickel, ex-governor.

Wally World
Virtual reality.

Week-on-week-off
A work schedule involving working one week, with the next off. Also, two-on, two-off, etc.

Wind chill
A calculation of relative cold involving wind speed combined with temperature.

Winter
Nine months of the year.

Yukon
The river; also Alaska's next door neighbor in Canada.

"Funny thing is you can substitute Alaska woman everyplace you have Alaska man and it would be absolutely true."

An Alaska man's comment when he read this book.

want more...

BOOK

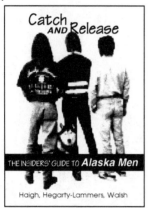

Catch and Release:
The Insiders' Guide to Alaska Men
by Haigh, Hegarty-Lammers, and Walsh

The insiders' guide to Alaska men by Alaska women tells of life in the north with this endangered species. A humorous guide book with attitude. Ridgetop Press $12.95.

T-SHIRT

Catch & Release T-Shirt

100% cotton short sleeve shirts. Two color design: Dogs saying: "Alaska Men, the odds are good.... but the goods are odd ! " or " I'm overly diversified and total unemployable ". Sizes: M / L / XL. Colors: Black or White. Crew neck: $16.00 or Jewel neck: $18.00.

TOUR

VanGo Tours:
"Experience Alaska"

Small group tours around Alaska offering the visitor an opportunity to: meet local people; learn about natural history, Native culture, Alaska lore; and see the sights. Summer tours include Wrangel St. Elias National Park, Denali, Yukon River. Winter trips to Yukon Quest & Iditarod sled dog races. Statewide escorted itineraries with guide, Pat Walsh.

TOUR

Midnight Fun Tours:
"Meet Me in Alaska"

Unique tours for women to experience the beauty of Alaska and meet men along the way. Tours organized around special events like a Christmas time holiday gala and summer celebrations in Alaska.

RIDGETOP PRESS / P.O. 1521 / HOMER, AK 99603 / TEL/FAX:907-235-5431

BOOK

Give Me the Hudson
or the Yukon
by Mike McCann

Mike is attuned to the hidden laugh in even grim situations. Life on a river in Alaska has never been presented this way. A collection of short stories of authors life on the Yukon and his growing up in New York. Ridgetop Press $9.00.

BOOK

Return to the River
by Mike McCann

McCann is one Alaskan who has been and seen and done. His sketches of notable characters and crazy doings are not only funny, they are true. A collection of short stories continuing where the first book left off. Ridgetop Press $11.95.

BOOK

Alaska Pioneer Interiors
by Jane Haigh

Cult classic. Collection of 80 archival photographs of Alaska Pioneer Home Interiors, 1903 - 1919 with detailed captions describing the furnishings in each room, and an introductory essay on the decorative arts of the period. Tanana-Yukon Historical Society. $16.95.

BOOK

Gold Rush Women
by Jane Haigh and Claire Murphy

Stories of the women who came North 100 years ago in the Klondike and Alaskan gold rushes. They came alone or with husbands, some in search of freedom, and all in a quest for their own definition of fortune. Includes stories of many women forgotten by the history books. Alaska Northwest Books $16.95.

RIDGETOP PRESS / P.O. 1521 / HOMER, AK 99603 / TEL/FAX:907-235-5431

send to ...

Mail order form **with payment** to:

RIDGETOP PRESS
P.O. 1521
HOMER, AK 99603

NAME (Please print)

ADDRESS

TELEPHONE /FAX

SEND PAYMENT VIA MONEY ORDER, CHECK OR CREDIT CARD:

VISA or MASTERCARD NUMBER (No other cards accepted)

EXPIRATION DATE

SIGNATURE

QUANTITY	TITLE	PRICE EACH	TOTALS
	Catch and Release: The Insiders' Guide to Alaska Men	$12.95	
	Give Me the Hudson or the Yukon	$ 9.00	
	Return to the River	$11.95	
	Alaska Pioneer Interiors	$16.95	
	Gold Rush Women	$16.95	
	Catch and Release T-Shirt (circle color choice / size / neckline / design) BLACK JEWEL *"Odds are..."* WHITE CREW M / L / XL *"Unemployable..."*	$16.00 $18.00	
	Add shipping and handling costs:	**per item** **$2.00**	
	TOTAL AMOUNT ENCLOSED:		

(check box)

☐ **I want to go on tour, send information:**
    VanGo Tours:
    "Experience Alaska"

☐ Midnight Fun Tours:
    "Meet Me in Alaska"

about the authors

Jane hiking in Denali.

JANE

Jane spends the long winter thinking up jokes to tell her friends and looking for the humor in every situation. She practices her oddball brand of improvisational performance art in her position on the local school board, and also writes serious books on Alaska history. She's lived in Fairbanks since she was 18 and has built her own house, twice. She's married to a guy with a good sense of humor and has two children.

"If it's not fun, why do it?"

KELLEY

Kelley lives and works in a dense, white birch forest in the Fairbanks hills with her gold miner husband, Doug Lammers, where they raise way cool labs. She travels all over Alaska in the course of her work as a community planning consultant, but makes sure that there's always time for one more outrageous adventure.

" Relax, Mom - it's fiction... purely fiction."

Kelley at home with her family.

PATRICIA

Pat's been here for twenty years, working as a graphic artist, customs inspector, fisherwoman, politcal organizer, and tour operator. She owns VanGo Tours. As is Fairbanks custom, she built an out-of-pocket house in the woods. She and her Alaska man travel around the state sharing adventures, like selling these books off the wings of a Cherokee 235.

"If it's for you, it won't pass you by."

Pat with a king salmon.